DATE DUE

ILL GSC 7732/8473		
2·9/99		

D1599907

DEMCO 38-297

The Making of
TANIA HEARST

The Making of
TANIA HEARST

DAVID BOULTON

NEW ENGLISH LIBRARY
TIMES MIRROR

45002351 6

Contents

Introduction

ON 14 November 1974 the American Attorney-General, William Saxbe, told a stunned press conference that he planned to make public details of FBI 'dirty tricks' authorised secretly over a fifteen year period by the Bureau's late director, J. Edgar Hoover.

The 'dirty tricks', said Saxbe, had been part of a counter-intelligence programme of the Federal Bureau of Investigation designed to disrupt or 'neutralise' organisations regarded as subversive. One trick was to manufacture evidence of immorality against radical leaders, but when that proved ineffective Hoover's men turned to more extreme methods. By the late 1960s they were running a string of sham organisations, ostensibly radical or revolutionary, with the aim of entrapment.

Saxbe didn't name the organisations, but he promised to give details to the Petersen Committee, set up to consider the legality, necessity and wisdom of 'abhorrent' operations. So the 'Feds', in an effort to polish up their tarnished reputation, had decided to come clean. The question now was whether local police departments would decide that, in the post-Watergate era, the time was also ripe for them to reveal the skeletons in their own cupboards.

Would police chief Davis in Los Angeles open the Los Angeles Police Department's own bulging bag of 'dirty tricks'?

He might begin by chronicling the support given by the LAPD to United Slaves, a black nationalist movement set up in opposition to the Panthers in the early 1960s. The United Slaves' symbol, a seven-headed cobra, was later adopted by the Symbionese Liberation Army. Davis might also speak frankly about the counter-intelligence work of his 'Black Desk' and its one-time operatives Louis Tackwood and Donald David DeFreeze. Tackwood had defected. DeFreeze had become 'field-marshal' of the SLA. The LAPD had kept its silence on both.

Coincidentally, on the very day Saxbe casually acknowledged that the Left's oft-repeated and much-derided conspiracy theories might after all have a factual basis, a twenty-seven-year-old girl who had been on the FBI's 'wanted' list for five years walked into the US Attorney's office in New York and gave herself up.

Jane Lauren Alpert, with her young lover, Samuel Melville, and her friend, Bernadine Dorhn, had been leaders of the Weathermen organisation which in 1969 planted a trail of bombs across New York in a desperate protest against the Vietnam war. Melville was caught and died in the Attica prison uprising in 1971. Bernadine Dorhn and Jane Alpert stayed on the run and became folk-heroines of the radical underground. They blazed a trail Patty Hearst was to follow five years later.

But life on the run affected Bernadine Dorhn and Jane Alpert in different ways. Dorhn's isolation seems to have hardened, even fossilised, her revolutionary commitment. But Jane Alpert, particularly after her lover's death, began to tire of disguises, whispered conversations, night runs – the claustrophobic life of a fugitive. On 14 November 1974 she gave herself up, saying she had grown older and wiser and was 'no longer in the grip of the mistaken ideology' which had caused her to flee.

Would Patty Hearst prove to be a Bernadine Dorhn or a Jane Alpert?

Saxbe's confessions and Jane Alpert's surrender are reminders that the strange case of the SLA, the story of how a black police spy and a rich white girl tried to start an American revolution, has depths which cannot yet be fully sounded and resonances which cannot yet be fully explained.

And it would be a mistake to see the story in the narrow perspectives of the American West. Britain watched with comparable horror the rise and fall of the Angry Brigade, led by young girls from decent middle-class families. Ulrike Meinhof led the Red Army Faction in guerilla warfare against the West German corporate state. 'The pen mightier than the sword?' she scoffed. 'What rubbish! The bomb is mightier than both.' In Dublin, Bridget Rose Dugdale, daughter of a wealthy businessman and art collector, was jailed for hijacking a helicopter and trying to bomb a police station in Strabane. Back in Britain the Home Secretary introduced 'draconian' anti-terrorist measures against the IRA bombers. This is the Age of the Terrorist. There is, and will continue to be, more than one Tania.

The intensity with which the world was gripped by the Patty Hearst story is not hard to understand. Almost every family today has its Patty, girl or boy, lost, stolen or strayed, dropped out, kicked out, left out or flipped out. And every smouldering ghetto of the underprivileged has its 'field-marshal' whose guns will liberate the people and whose communiqués, written in blood, spit out the battle orders.

The story of Patty Hearst and the SLA is a microcosm of the huge conflicts that threaten to tear our world apart: rich against poor, strong against weak, black against white, young against old, women against men, old against new, cops against robbers, dreams against experience. Here they are all rolled up in a single neat wrapping, stamped with the haunting image of a lovely girl in thespian pose, carbine in hand, poised to kill but demanding love, her backdrop a seven-headed cobra.

1 Citizen Kane's Granddaughter

HILLSBOROUGH, California, can hardly be called a town. It is rather a complex of hidden retreats for wealthy corporation presidents and executives who commute each day into San Francisco, twenty miles north. In contrast to Beverley Hills, its equivalent community in Los Angeles, Hillsborough is decently reticent and unostentatious. Bing Crosby has a house there, but he's the only show business resident. His neighbours are modest millionaires whose names mean little to the outside world. It's the banks, businesses and cartels they run which are household names.

Not that Hillsborough likes to be thought of as exclusive in these sensitive, egalitarian times. The 'city manager', hired to supervise services for the 2764 homes sprawled on six square miles of landscaped hills, is at pains to assure enquiring strangers: 'We've got coloured people living here, Chinese people, Asian, everything.' His police chief, commanding a private force of twenty-five men who rarely have to deal with any crime more novel or exciting than the routine burglary, confirms Hillsborough's racial tolerance but reveals all when he says, 'If you're black and you have a couple of million in your pocket, join the club.'

Santa Inez Avenue runs through the very centre of this enclave of wealth, curling up into hills which give spectacular

views over the lower half of San Francisco Bay. Like most Hillsborough streets, it has no public path, just a succession of
private driveways winding through the Californian oaks, pines
and eucalyptus trees which keep the heated pools, hard tennis
courts and the houses themselves at least half-hidden from
strangers and neighbours.

At the foot of West Santa Inez is the Hearst house. Randolph
Apperson Hearst never liked to have it described as a mansion.
And now the word has been proscribed in his eight newspapers
and on his seven radio and television stations. House or
mansion, its twenty-two rooms are fronted by a Georgian-style
entrance flanked by Greek columns and a forest of well tended
potted orchids. Inside, the 4000 square feet of Persian-carpeted
living space is twice the minimum permitted area laid down by a
city ordinance designed to discourage the mere middle-rich. The
general impression is one of well-ordered calm, a dignified
affluence without opulence.

Hearst money, like all the best Californian wealth, was dug
out of the ground. Randolph's grandfather, George Hearst, was
one of the Forty-niners who had joined in the great gold rush.
After ten years of digging he had struck silver. Thereafter, it
seemed he couldn't put his spade to the ground without turning
up a fortune. With more millions than he could count, and still
illiterate as the day he had gone West, he had bought himself a
Senate seat and an ailing newspaper, the *San Francisco
Examiner.*

George Hearst started the Hearst legend, but it was his son,
the great William Randolph Hearst, who carried it to its heights
and made the name Hearst one of the most awesome and most
hated in America.

William Randolph Hearst began his stupendous career by
seizing control of the *Examiner* from his father and conning
seven-and-a-half million dollars from his mother. Then, with a
ruthlessness that was astonishing even for turn-of-the-century
America, he began to revolutionise American journalism by
marketing a sensational diet of boldly-packaged murder,
adultery and multiple shock.

Orson Welles' *Citizen Kane* was modelled on William

Randolph Hearst, but the mighty Kane was but a pale reflection of the real Citizen Hearst – 'the Chief'. He made as much news as he reported, often with even more panache. His crazed jingoism was instrumental in taking America to the brink of war with Spain. In politics he destroyed every cause he supported. He even visited a promising young European statesman named Adolf Hitler and advised him how best to proceed in order to win friends for National Socialism in the United States. He became one of the great film moguls. Nonetheless, it was his network of newspapers and magazines which remained at the heart of his vast business empire.

Yet it wasn't his journalism, nor his politics, nor even the scandals of his not-so-private life which made Hearst a household name. What delighted his handful of admirers and fed the rage of his millions of detractors was the unparalleled extravagance of his life-style. It was to describe William Randolph Hearst that the phrase 'the last of the big spenders' was coined. And the great extravagance of his life was Hearst Castle at San Simeon.

Hearst Castle was the last of the world's great follies. Built high in the hills between the Pacific and the Santa Lucia Mountains, its ivory-coloured towers overlooked a 240,000 acre ranch that stretched fifty miles along one of the most beautiful coastlines in the world. Still unfinished at the Chief's death in 1951, it contained thirty-eight bedrooms, thirty-one bathrooms, fourteen sitting-rooms, a cinema and two libraries. Guests were housed in three adjacent mini-castles containing another forty-six rooms. A marble pool with a Graeco-Roman temple façade and Etruscan-style colonades enhanced America's most extravagant private home. In the grounds was kept a priceless collection of exotic monkeys, cheetahs, lions, leopards and panthers. On the walls of the castle were tapestries, paintings and objets d'art from all over the world. In the cellars, unopened crates held more priceless treasures for which, despite those acres of space, there simply wasn't room upstairs.

All through the inter-war depression years, Hearst played host to movie stars and starlets, writers, artists, princes and politicians. While half of California struggled to survive, Hearst lived it up in a continuous non-stop orgy of conspicuous consumption. To the poor, particularly the organised, conscious poor, the name Hearst was high in the lexicon of demonology. When Citizen Hearst proved mortal the legend clung to his name, and stank.

Control of his empire passed at his death to his sons, of whom Randolph was reckoned the most businesslike. Much of the wealth was channelled into a charitable foundation, which avoided crippling death duties. Randolph became chairman of the Hearst Foundation, valued then at $43 million and now at $80 million. San Simeon Castle was turned over to the State of California to become second only to Disneyland as the biggest tourist attraction on the American continent.

A quiet, conservative man, Randolph Hearst did all he could to shake off his father's Citizen Kane tag. He avoided public extravagance and for most of the year kept himself and his family fairly successfully hidden away in Hillsborough, well out of the gaze of the press.

He had married a Southern beauty, Catherine Campbell: wealthy, conservative and Catholic. He himself had converted to Catholicism to please her, but religion never assumed the central place in his life that it had held from the start in hers. Randolph and Catherine Hearst had four daughters: Ann, Vicki, Virginia and Patricia Campbell, whom they called Patty.

There was nothing in the uneventful life of this sedate, respectable family to suggest the violent sensations on which their wealth was founded. And there was nothing to suggest that the most violent sensation of all was yet to come.

Patty's life was much like that of any girl born into rich Californian society: comfortably undramatic, uneventful, unremarkable, a five-star childhood followed by no more than a hint of fashionable teenage rebellion. There are few clues in those first nineteen years to the extraordinary metamorphosis of 1974.

Her mother saw to it that Patty had a Catholic education and she took her first communion when she was eight. The family album shows her, hands clasped demurely, head and shoulders draped in conventional white lace, and an impiously cheeky smile on her soap-commercial face.

Friends of her own age in Hillsborough remember Patty as a quiet, cautious little girl, happy to join in junior swimming and tennis at the Burlingame Country Club, but precociously disapproving of wilder games. She was sent to a succession of private elementary schools. After St Matthews in San Mateo and Sacred Heart in Menlo Park – both as unremittingly Catholic in their ways as her mother – she went to the undenominational Crystal Springs school in Hillsborough. Her teachers remember her early years there, before 1968. 'She was very bright, very mature.' says one. 'She craved to be loved, to get attention,' recalls another. One teacher describes her as 'bull-headed'. At fourteen she was already noted for her maturity and her preference for the company of older children and adults, a dependence on the experience of others which perhaps reflected a sense of emptiness in her own childhood.

In the autumn of 1968 Patty Hearst left home for the first time in order to become a boarder at Santa Catalina, an exclusive Catholic prep school for girls in Monterey, nearly a hundred miles down the Pacific coast. Here her education and social training were in the hands of Dominican nuns who, since they couldn't teach her the virtue of poverty, concentrated on chastity and obedience. During Patty's first term a friend was expelled, allegedly for holding hands with another girl. The nuns called it 'carnal contact' and for weeks the whole school was made to feel that the wrath of God was about to be loosed on Monterey's own little Sodom and Gomorrah.

But Santa Catalina bred its rebels, and Patty was soon one. She found her first boyfriend, Stanley Dollar, the sixteen-year-old son of a steamship millionaire who was attending the Robert Louis Stevenson Boys' School down the road. They exchanged secret letters regularly until the day when young Stanley Dollar wrote enthusiastically about his discovery of pot and flower-power. But Patty's rebellion didn't go that far. She wrote back saying she found the hippie cult appalling. 'There is no hope for me in this "turned on" generation,' she told her young suitor primly.

Nevertheless, Patty was growing up fast. The following year she left Santa Catalina suddenly and in mysterious circumstances. Today both her family and the school will say no more than that Patty asked to leave and her father agreed to take her away. Later reports suggested she had been expelled for smoking pot but this was denied. What did happen? Patty was eventually to confide in the man who became her fiancé that she had had her first lover at the age of fourteen, a man of twenty-six who had been her 'sexual teacher'. Deeply shocked, her parents brought her back to Crystal Springs at Hillsborough where they could keep a closer eye on her.

At Crystal Springs she met a mathematics and philosophy teacher named Steven Weed. He didn't teach Patty's class, but by the spring of 1970, as Patty entered her final year, she made it plain to her friends that she had her sights set on Mr Weed. She was seventeen, he just twenty-four.

By the summer they were seeing each other regularly, but discreetly: teachers were not supposed to fall for the pupils. Then further scandal was averted when Patty persuaded her parents to let her finish schooling at Menlo College, a private school that was running with the times by opening its doors to women. The romance was then free to flower in the open.

Patty found it easier to mix with older friends in Steven's age group than with people of her own age. Her schoolfriends tended to find her distant and stand-offish, her teachers thought her mature and self-confident. She came top of the class, doing particularly well in biology, art history and photography. But, fashionably, Patty refused a formal debutante's coming-out which upset her mother. Then, at the end-of-term banquet, she told her parents she was going to leave home to live with Steve.

Mrs Hearst took it badly, protesting that Patty couldn't possibly marry a man with a name like Weed and a toothbrush moustache. The liberated daughter patiently explained that she had no intention of *marrying* Steven, she merely intended to live with him. 'No one gets married these days,' she told her horrified mother.

Catherine Hearst tried scheming. She set about arranging a place for Patty at Stanford University when the campus was still quiet, conservative and relatively untouched by student rebellion, and where Patty would be a safe distance from the noxious Weed. But Patty wasn't having that. She was going to Berkeley.

The University of California campus at Berkeley had for a full decade been the mecca of radical student politics. The great 'Free Speech Movement' of the early 1960s had begun on this vast, sprawling site on the hills overlooking the east side of San Francisco Bay. Youth counter-culture and the rhetoric of revolution had incubated together at Berkeley. And when the white, middle-class, radicalised students, fired with fury over Vietnam and civil rights, linked up with the black revolutionaries in neighbouring Oakland, the resultant symbiosis – though the word had yet to become fashionable – was enough to set the Reagan generation reaching for its guns.

Catherine Hearst, as it happened, was a member of the University's Board of Regents, appointed by ex-movie star Governor Reagan. She knew Berkeley only too well. Time and again the Board had been mauled in combat with successive student bodies. Mrs Hearst's regency was marked by an impeccably conservative voting record, but while that helped keep university investments in South Africa and out of Cuba it didn't make for trouble-free administration. At almost all costs, Mrs Hearst didn't want any of her daughters, least of all the wilful Patty, to go to Berkeley. But she knew better than to seek a head-on clash. She bided her time and chose the moment to suggest Patty took a summer cruise to Europe to 'think things over'. Patty had no intention of thinking things over, but she liked the idea of a cruise. Off she went to Greece for six weeks. Meanwhile Steven Weed rented a one-bedroom apartment at 2603 Bienvenue Avenue, Berkeley, and enrolled both himself and his girl at the university.

Patty returned and moved straight into the apartment with Steve. Her father told her that her behaviour was deplorable, but nevertheless gave the lovers a set of dishes as a token of his continuing affection. Mrs Hearst was more deeply upset The impropriety of the affair scandalised her Catholic conscience and threatened her social standing. Moreover, the cruise had made no difference whatever to Patty's determination to go to Berkeley rather than Stanford.

First, however, like so many other similarly-placed children of the rich, Patty wanted to assert her independence by earning money of her own. She deferred her enrolment at Berkeley to the winter term and started a job at Capwell's department store in Oakland, earning $2.25 an hour taking Christmas card orders. A little shy perhaps of her wealthy background, she told no one at the store who she was, and her customers had no cause to know they were ordering their cards from the granddaughter of William Randolph Hearst.

After Christmas Patty began classes at Berkeley, intending to major in art history. Her father gave her an allowance of $300 a month and an open credit card, so with Steven's earnings from teaching they lived comfortably enough. She never talked about her family's wealth. Maybe she took it for granted. Maybe she had already begun to be a little ashamed of it.

With the winding-down of the Vietnam war and the exhausted disintegration of the peace movement, the political scene on the campus wasn't what it had been in the blissful optimistic dawn of the Students for a Democratic Society, the Chicago Seven and the multi-factional New Left. Patty and Steve, by all accounts, avoided politics. They had supported McGovern in 1972, but in the 1973 student elections they voted against the radical slate. 'We were apolitical,' Weed told enquiring newsmen a year later. 'We didn't even subscribe to a newspaper. There's something about Berkeley and politics. You're either in it or out of it. We turned away from any interest in politics.'

Steve and Patty did not however stand wholly aloof from the relaxed, iconoclastic life-style of the campus. If they avoided the Jesus-freakery and assorted mysticisms which were filling the vacuum left by the retreat of political activism, they were Berkeley conformists in at least one respect: they were regularly smoking pot.

Soft drugs could be bought easily enough in Berkeley or Oakland. One ready source of supply was a girl who sold orange juice at a stand called Fruity Rudy's on the edge of the campus. The girl's name was Nancy Ling Perry, and although Steven

Weed has no recollection of her, she seems to have been acquainted with him since his name and telephone number were listed in her diary. Certainly Nancy was soon to come to know Patty very well indeed.

Patty and Steve had lived together for eighteen months when they decided they would, after all, get married. This led to a happy reconciliation with Patty's mother who had never faltered in her daily prayers that the man she persisted in calling 'Toothbrush' would either make an honest woman of her daughter or just go away. Patty and Steven joined the family for Christmas 1973 at their ski-resort home in Wyntoon, where they formally celebrated their engagement. From there, Patty took her fiancé to the castle at San Simeon where they surveyed the art treasures of grandfather Hearst and plotted how best to appropriate one or two for the new home they planned to buy later in 1974.

In the new year Patty and her mother began a series of shopping trips to select china and silverware for the bottom drawer. Randolph Hearst bought his daughter a new sports car. The engagement was announced in the appropriate columns of all the right newspapers.

Patty's rebellion, it seemed, was over. She had grown out of it, Mrs Hearst told herself with quiet satisfaction. The mother was not to know what powerful urges, what intimations of liberation and independence her daughter was bottling up inside her. Nor could she have any notion of the violence of the coming explosion.

In January 1974 Patty told her father that his *Examiner* was a stuffy, irrelevant newspaper which no one under eighty read. She finished an essay on Rubens and handed it over to her art history tutor who gave it an A-plus and put it in his desk ready to return it to her the following week.

Neither the Hearsts nor the tutor ever saw Patty again.

2   Genesis of an Army

WHILE Patty and Steve settled into their life together in the
Bienvenue Avenue apartment, half in and half out of Berkeley
student society, others around them were creating what was to
become the Symbionese Liberation Army.

Nancy Ling was a furniture dealer's daughter from Santa
Rosa, sixty miles north of San Francisco. The Lings were card-
carrying Republicans, comfortably off, living insulated lives in
a small middle-class town. Similar backgrounds generally pro-
duce children who are the mirror image of their parents; in this
case, it produced a revolutionary.

At Junior High School, Nancy was given her first leadership
role – as a cheerleader. In High School she was active in the
Girls' League. When her father canvassed in 1964 for Barry
Goldwater, Nancy canvassed with him. She was barely
seventeen.

'Nancy was always one for a cause', remembered her father
later. So with a thirst for better causes than Goldwater's, Nancy
left Whittier, the Los Angeles suburban college where Nixon
had once been a pupil, and went to Berkeley to study English
literature. That was in September 1966. She was by then nineteen years old and just 4ft 11in tall.

Nancy Ling found her new cause within weeks. That autumn
the Vietnam war came to Berkeley when a team of Navy

recruiters set up a stall in the student union block. The Berkeley chapter of Students for a Democratic Society placed their own stall alongside it and handed out anti-war literature.

Student union officials demanded that the recruiting officers take their stall elsewhere. University administrators, backed by a majority of regents including Catherine Hearst, demanded that the SDS pull out. Neither side budged and anti-war students escalated the clash by holding a sit-in round the Navy stall. The administration sent in the local police to arrest the demonstrators' leaders (who included the rising New Left superstar, Jerry Rubin). The student association responded by calling an all-out strike which would last five days before ending on promise of a joint student-faculty commission of enquiry.

For five days America's biggest university was paralysed over Vietnam. For Nancy Ling, who joined the sit-in round the Navy table, it was her first taste of protest politics, her baptism into the fellowship that was remorselessly to strip her of her conservative middle-class values.

Student radicalism was only one input factor in the making of the new Nancy. Spring and summer 1967 were the time when the Bay Area was engulfed in a frenzy of flower power. San Francisco's Haight-Ashbury district became the youth capital of the world. There were free clinics, free food programmes, expensive dope. It was a very different world from the prim cosiness of Santa Rosa, only an hour's drive away.

Nancy discovered soul music and graduated to black culture. She met Gilbert Scott Perry, a black jazz pianist. Between gigs he was working for the California Department of Employment in Oakland, and she came to his counter looking for a vacation job. She landed both a job and Perry. The black man was 6ft 2in to her 4ft 11in. They were married on Boxing Day 1967 in the First Unitarian Church, Kensington, California – a sop to her unhappy parents. Thereafter, through what proved to be a stormy on-off marriage, Nancy called herself Nancy Ling Perry.

In 1968 the year of the flower gave way to the year of the pig. President Johnson announced his forthcoming political suicide, Martin Luther King and Robert Kennedy were assassinated and the Black Panthers built up their mass following in

Oakland. Haight-Ashbury was overrun by pimps, porn-merchants and sleaze. In Topanga Canyon, Los Angeles, Charles Manson, self-proclaimed God of Fuck, was recruiting his harem of rich white girls, destroying their old values and training them for eventual ritual murder. In Berkeley the student Left was sick from self-inflicted wounds. There were more sit-ins and faculty occupations, but they were increasingly factional and divisive. No one remembers Nancy taking part this time.

In 1970 Nancy graduated with a BA in literature. In April, apparently politicised again, she travelled with the large Berkeley contingent to Washington for the massive student demonstration on the lawns of the White House protesting against the extension of the Vietnam war into Cambodia and the killing by National Guards of Kent State students. Somewhere in the crowd, still unknown to each other, were at least four of Nancy's future comrades in the SLA.

Nancy decided to stay in the Bay Area after graduating instead of returning home to Santa Rosa. She had developed a taste for excitement, for easy kicks, and like many of her contemporaries she began to rationalise her growing alienation from conventional society with the language of revolution. In a letter to an old schoolfriend she wrote that living in San Francisco gave her 'easy access to crime'. Nancy bought the current slogan that private property couldn't be stolen, only liberated; so she liberated library books, records, a pool table and a stereo set. She was never caught.

Again like many of her generation, Nancy held her academic qualification as of little value. Most of her future comrades in the SLA deliberately took working-class jobs on graduating and Nancy became a topless go-go dancer at a North Beach tourist joint. 'She was quite an attraction,' says the manager, 'with those tiny tits bobbing about just three feet off the ground.' But Nancy preached revolution to the other girls, and when they complained she was fired.

Again she seemed for a time to lose interest in politics. The girl who had shouted for Goldwater, sat down for peace in Vietnam, liberated library books to prove her revolutionary commitment and tried to ferment a go-go strike, seemed suddenly to be consumed by a succession of esoteric interests: yoga, transcendental meditation, I Ching, astrology, Indian religion and the Egyptian occult. Strands of some of these cultish obsessions were to find their way into the bizarre pot-pourri of SLA literature and symbolism.

Still looking for causes, Nancy discovered women's liberation. Her marriage with Gilbert Perry began to break up She took a succession of black lovers, including a Panther from Oakland whom she later denounced with characteristic arbitrariness as an FBI agent. She moved into the drugs scene, graduating from pot to opium and LSD. Nancy was soon known as a reliable source from whom stuff could be got in a hurry.

By the summer of 1972 she was one of Berkeley's street children, hanging around the campus as if to cling to youth and freedom. She started selling fruit juice from a campus stall and fell in love with the stall's black owner, Rudy Henderson. She signed up for a course in chemistry – another passing interest which she would later put to the service of the revolution.

Towards the end of 1972 she began an affair with another black man, Chris Thompson, who ran a vegetable stall called Harlem on My Mind. 'She was wild, but nice', Thompson told reporters later. And it was Thompson who introduced the wild, nice girl, still searching for causes, to the friends who would join her in building a Symbionese Federation of Nations and a Symbionese Liberation Army.

Thompson's friends lived in a large, rambling house at 5939 Chabot Road, Berkeley. An aspiring jazz musician named Dave Gunnell had bought it in 1970 as a base for the great band he dreamed of forming.

The band never materialised, but the house acquired lodgers. Gunnell and his Chinese-American girl friend, Jean Chan, ran a Chinese food stand on the Berkeley campus not far from Fruity Rudy's orange juice stall and Harlem on My Mind. The stand was called 'Peking Man' and 5939 Chabot Road came to be known as Peking House. The name had a deliberate, provocative ambiguity since Gunnell and his lodgers belonged to a Bay Area Maoist group called Venceremos ('We shall conquer').

In 1971, down to Berkeley from Allentown, Pennsylvania, came Willie Wolfe, a young pacifist who so hated violence that he had persuaded his wealthy anaesthetist father to sell his hunting rifles. His friends called him 'Willie the Wolf' and he came to Berkeley to do a Black Studies course. He answered a 'rooms vacant' advertisement and took up lodgings at Peking House.

The following year a new couple moved in. They were Russell Jack Little and his girl friend, Robyn Steiner. Little was a working-class white Southerner from Florida, a self-confessed red-necked racist until in 1969, at the University of Florida, he came under the influence of a young Marxist tutor and 'got hip to the economics of capitalism'. In the summer of 1972 the couple drove up to the Bay Area where they thought the action was, taking the room in Peking House next to Willie Wolfe.

Wolfe's tutor in Black Studies at Berkeley was a large, extrovert black professor, Colston Westbrook. Westbrook was coordinator of the Black Cultural Association which ran twice-weekly classes for black prisoners in Vacaville jail, an hour's drive south of San Francisco. Vacaville is described as a 'medical facility'. Nine hundred prisoners, black and white, are there for 'psychological evaluation', in which the BCA's classes were intended to play an informal part.

In the wake of the Attica jail revolt, the killing of George Jackson and the Angela Davis case, black prisoners in San Quentin, Soledad and Vacaville had come to organise themselves in what were often avowedly revolutionary groups. Revolutionary rhetoric made a strong appeal to prisoners. Their own violent actions could be rationalised by a theory of black repression and justified as proper retribution against an oppressive white society. The most vicious act of personal violence could be elevated to a social duty, or at least an inevitable historical reflex. So revolution gave prison life a meaning and a perspective of hope.

To dilute the more intense forms of political expression in Vacaville, to drain off hostile energies and perhaps to make prisoners' groups more susceptible to official control, the Black Cultural Association was opened up to allow outside visitors to come in and mix with the prisoners in what prison officials intended to be organised tutorials. In 1971, shortly after moving into Peking House, Willie Wolfe applied through Westbrook to go on the BCA visiting list and was accepted.

Friends said the experience 'blew his mind'. A quiet middle-class boy, an earnest pacifist, was suddenly plunged into the extraordinary sub-culture of a black prison with its arcane rituals and language. It seemed to him, as it had to so many white radicals of his generation, that here in the black prisons were the potential makers of the American revolution, the wretched of the earth with nothing to lose.

Willie recruited his friends from the Chabot Road collective. Dave Gunnell and Jean Chan, Russell Little and Robyn Steiner were all accepted as prison visitors under the auspices of Westbrook and the BCA.

So every Friday night the young radicals from Peking House trooped down to Vacaville for a Black Culture rap session. The meetings took a bizarre form, a mixture of Black Muslim rituals, 'back-to-Africa' incantations and Black Panther Marxism. There was a flag ceremony at which the tricolour of the 'Republic of New Africa' was paraded to the accompaniment of tribal music and black power salutes. This was followed by readings and discussions, first on 'black consciousness' and eventually on the mechanics of guerrilla war. Westbrook waved aside the alarm of the prison administration at this influx of radicals. It was good therapy for the prisoners, he said, and would 'bring the radicals down to earth'. The prison chief, Robert Procunier, was reluctantly persuaded to turn a blind eye to the strange activities in his hospital-prison.

Peking House was absorbed in this new and potent interest when Chris Thompson brought his new girlfriend, Nancy Ling Perry, into the circle. She too became an accredited prison visitor, giving herself with characteristic thoroughness to the cause of the prison reform movement and her new friends.

When Thompson dropped out for a time she began an affair with Russell Little. And when Thompson resumed the visiting, he brought along his new girlfriend. Her name was Mizmoon.

The girl everyone came to call Mizmoon was born Patricia Monique Soltysik, daughter of a prosperous chemist in the small seaside town of Goleta, ten miles north of Santa Barbara, California. One of seven children, she made her mark at Dos Pueblos High School where she became treasurer of the student senate and president of the Usherettes Service Organisation. In 1968 she was awarded an academic scholarship to the University of California and became a child of Berkeley.

That same year her parents were divorced. It was a traumatic experience which affected her deeply. But Patricia had learned from her mother a positive philosophy which saw obstacles as existing only to be overcome. 'Men can live to the fullest only by observing an optimistic attitude', she wrote in a school essay before leaving for Berkeley, adding, 'The pessimist will live only the life of a fugitive.'

Patricia arrived in Berkeley in 1968, the year of student revolutions. 'Some people can live in Berkeley and come out of it unscathed; others are consumed by it,' said her brother, Frederick. 'Patricia was consumed by it. Hers was not an evolution, it was an explosion. I tried to show her that Berkeley wore its blinkers, that Berkeley wasn't the hub of the universe, not even the hub of California. She didn't hear me.'

Patricia took an apartment in Channing Way, part of the student quarter where slogans like 'Gay Power', 'Love Yourself' and 'Eat the Rich' decorate the walls. Then in 1972 she abruptly dropped out of university to devote herself to the women's movement and to revolution. Deciding that revolutionaries must mix with the working class, she took a job as a janitor in the Berkeley Public Library.

By this time she had openly acknowledged her bisexuality and had become the lover of the girl who addressed her as 'Ms Moon'. Camilla Christine Hall was the dumpy, short-sighted daughter of the Rev George Hall, a Lutheran minister from Minneapolis. Camilla spent her childhood in the mission fields of Latin America and Africa before being sent in 1963 to the University of Minnesota. There, before it became a fashionable cause, she threw herself into work for women's rights and after graduating with a degree in humanities took a full-time job as a social worker advising unmarried mothers. The girl they had called Candy at home was now known as 'Miss Positive Action'. However her social work remained apolitical until, in 1970, drawn by the magic that cast its spell over so many of her generation, she moved to Berkeley.

There, in Channing Way, Camilla Hall met Patricia Soltysik and they began what was to be a three-year-long love affair. For Camilla, 'Mizmoon' was her only love and she poured out her heart in passionate verse:

> I will cradle you
>   in my woman's hips
> Kiss you
>   with my woman's lips
> Fold you
>   to my heart and sing:
> Sister woman
>   you are a joy to me.

Patricia responded by legally changing her name to Mizmoon. Camilla was drawn into her lover's revolutionary politics and abandoned her social work to take a working-class job as a gardener in one of Berkeley's parks. By the end of 1972 she had followed Mizmoon into the cause of black prisoners, on the road that would lead to the SLA.

Angela De Angelis was known to her friends and family as 'Angel'. Like Patty Hearst she had a Catholic upbringing. Like Nancy Ling Perry she was a school cheerleader. Unlike both, her background was working class. Her father was an official in Local 999 of the Teamsters Union. Angela's mother died when she was fourteen, but like any self-respecting American working man, Lawrence De Angelis made sure his daughter had a good middle-class education.

Manchester Regional High School, New Jersey, had never had an anti-war demonstration, never admitted a black student, never had a youth culture. It was the right place for 'Angel'. She became captain of the cheerleaders, president of the drama society, a delegate to the American Legion's Girls' State convention. 'She floated through the halls followed by admiring friends and enamoured hangers-on' says a school friend, Michael Wolff. 'Angel existed as an ornament', says one of her boy friends, Harris Weiner. 'She was the receptacle of people's ideas of what an All-American Girl was supposed to be. And she dug it, she dug herself.'

In September 1966 Angela enrolled in the safely respectable University of Indiana at Bloomington. She entered a beauty contest, came second and made up for it by winning the part of the Virgin Mary in a passion play. Later, while playing Perdida in *The Winter's Tale*, she fell for a sharp-featured youth among the extras, Gary Atwood.

Even Bloomington had its radicals and Atwood was an active member of the Trotskyist Young Socialist Alliance. Angel, hitherto wholly apolitical, was drawn into a circle of Marxist studies and anti-war rap sessions. Among Gary's political friends were Bill Harris and Emily Schwartz.

Harris, stepson of a US Air Force colonel in Carmel, Indiana, had enrolled at Bloomington in 1964, stayed one year, then joined the Marine Corps and was posted to Da Nang. He was one of the many who were radicalised by first-hand experience of fighting the Viet Cong. When he finally returned to Indiana University in 1967 he became active in Vietnam Veterans Against the War, a peace movement which put many embittered ex-soldiers on the escalator to revolutionary politics.

His girlfriend, Emily Schwartz, daughter of a rich consulting engineer in Clarendon Hills near Chicago, had just obtained a Bachelor's degree in English and was staying on at Bloomington to do a teacher's course. She was already a disciple of Women's Lib and the New Left.

Harris was one of hundreds who came back from the 1968

Chicago Democratic Convention with bandages on his head to bind the wounds left by Mayor Daley's uniformed and licensed rioters. Bill, Emily, Gary and Angela, drawn together by mutual political interests, argued about the demonstration. Gary thought it adventurist, elitist and a hostage to reaction. Bill believed it would radicalise the masses and open their eyes to the reality of State violence. The same arguments were being tossed back and forth in similar groups, large and small, across the whole spectrum of the American Left and its observers.

Bill became excited by the Black Panthers and talked of throwing up 'useless study' to live and work in Oakland where the Panthers had their strongest base. Emily organised food and clothing drives for the poor, covering the walls of her apartment with pictures of starving children. Angela, younger and less intellectually developed than her friends, worked hard to catch up. When the National Guard shot down the Kent State students in 1970 she wore a black armband to the school where she was working as part of a trainee teacher course. When she refused to take it off she was fired. It was the end of her teaching career.

Bill Harris and Emily Schwartz were married in 1970; Gary Atwood and Angela De Angelis in 1971.

Disillusioned by the collapse of the revolutionary student movement, the debacle of McCarthy–McGovern liberalism and the clear dawning of the age of Richard Nixon, the newly-wed Harrises copped out and went off on an extended trip to North Africa. When they returned in December Gary Atwood was in the throes of crisis over his impending call to military service. Bill said on no account should he go, nor should he 'lend credibility to the system' by formally applying for CO status: he should simply refuse. Gary pointed out that this could mean an indeterminate period in jail, which he and Angela wished to avoid. Eventually, against Harris's advice, Gary applied for recognition as a conscientious objector. When, to his surprise, recognition was granted, he and Angela arranged to move to the Bay Area to do alternative service in community work.

The Harrises followed a few months later, enticed by the

Atwoods's glowing accounts of life in Berkeley. The four were soon arguing about politics again. Gary was by now a hard-line Trotskyist, imbued in and forever quoting the texts of Marx, Lenin and the founder of the Fourth International. To Bill and Emily and, increasingly, to Angela, this was the arid politics of the Old Left. They matched Gary's quotes with their own from trendier luminaries – Mao, Guevara and Debray. Relationships began to be strained.

The argument was essentially about the uses of violence. Gary argued for the politics of the long haul, the need to pursue a programme which would concentrate on 'raising the consciousness of the masses' to the point at which they themselves would make the revolution. Bill, Emily and Angela wanted the revolution now. The consciousness of the masses was raised by *making* revolution, they argued, not by postponing it. A small group of dedicated revolutionaries could light the spark that would set the whole forest ablaze.

In the spring of 1973, riven by this kind of dissension, the Atwoods's marriage broke up. Angela moved in with the Harrises and threw in her lot with their like-minded friends. Through Emily she became more deeply involved in radical feminism and met Camilla Hall and Mizmoon. Through them she joined the revolutionary circle in Vacaville jail. Symbiosis wasn't far on the road ahead.

The convict who shone as the brightest star in Vacaville's Black Cultural Association was a twenty-eight-year-old black named Donald David DeFreeze.

The man who would soon be 'field-marshal' of the SLA was one of eight children born to a toolmaker and a nurse in Cleveland, Ohio. His home background could scarcely be more different from that of his white prison visitors. A state psychiatrist wrote of him in 1965, when he had been arrested for possession of a shotgun, a knife and home-made bomb:

DeFreeze states father tried to kill him three times. Used to inflict inhuman punishment – hit him with hammers, baseball bats, etc. He shows areas on head where he was struck and had to receive sutures. Every time he went to the hospital, his father told them he just got hurt. The time he was picked up with the gun, he had planned to shoot father who had been mistreating him.

'The time he was picked up with a gun' was the occasion of his first arrest when he was just fourteen. Five years later, in 1963, he met and married Gloria Thomas, a divorced mother of three. Barely a year later he was in court for deserting his family. In 1965, after a reconciliation, he took them west to Los Angeles where they settled in the Compton district, south of Watts.

That year Watts erupted in one of the worst race riots ever seen in any American city. By that time Donald DeFreeze had discovered a new role. He had become a petty informer for the Los Angeles Police Department.

The use of informers, paid either by cash or by promise of immunity, is standard police practice in Los Angeles, as almost everywhere. DeFreeze, with his knowledge of the ghetto underworld and his taste for adventure, was a useful catch. He joined a stable of informers run from the police department 'Black Desk'.

DeFreeze didn't let his work for the police interfere with his own freelance activities in crime. On 9 June 1967 he was crossing Los Angeles on his wife's bicycle when he was stopped by police for ignoring a red light. The policeman was surprised to find in the basket on the handlebars two bombs and a pistol. DeFreeze was charged on two counts of unlawful possession of explosives and one of carrying a concealed weapon. Although still on probation for his 1965 offence, he wasn't jailed. Instead, his probation was merely extended to 14 September 1970.

Two months after the bicycle incident, on 2 December, DeFreeze was arrested again, this time for robbing and beating a prostitute, but he escaped on the way to the police station. Surprisingly, the charge was later dropped.

The gun used by DeFreeze in this escapade proved to have come from a cache of 200 stolen a few days earlier from a local surplus store. DeFreeze had carried out the robbery with a partner, Ronald Coleman. After his arrest, escape and recapture, DeFreeze switched back to his informer's role and shopped his friend. Coleman went to jail. DeFreeze, astonishingly, was released on bail. A Department of Corrections psychiatrist's report described him as ' . . . an emotionally confused and conflicting young man with deep-rooted feelings of inadequacy. His disorganisation and impaired social adjustment seem to suggest a schizophrenic potential. He seems to have a fascination with regard to firearms and explosives . . . which makes him dangerous.'

Dangerous or not, the police department *continued* to run him as an informer. Clearly his anti-social, criminal characteristics were not considered an obstacle to his work. And DeFreeze continued to play his own game, being arrested again in April 1968 for burglary. Maybe there was insufficient evidence against him; maybe his police work saved him again. For whatever reason, he was *once again released* without charge.

Two months later on 5 June 1968, Robert Kennedy was shot dead in the Ambassador Hotel, Los Angeles. To the Los Angeles police it was the night they were caught napping. One immediate result was a shake-up in the police department. District Attorney Evelle J. Younger, soon to be elevated to State Attorney-General, in which role he would play a prominent part in the Hearst affair, set up an elite police corps called Special Unit Senator (SUS). When the Kennedy investigation was complete, SUS was merged with other elements of police intelligence to form a new department, the Criminal Conspiracy Section (CCS).

Something of the inner workings of CCS – its use of informers, entrapment procedures and *agents provocateur* – is known from the confessions or allegations of Louis E. Tackwood, a black CCS operative who defected to the radical movement in 1971. Tackwood told his story in a series of tape-recorded interviews with a group of Leftist writers and lawyers, the Citizens Research and Investigation Committee, which published them in a book, *The Glasshouse Tapes.*

According to Tackwood his own first assignment for CCS, to which he was transferred after several years as a common informer, was liaison between the police and a black nationalist organisation called United Slaves, led by Ron Karenga. His second assignment was to watch and 'help create conspiracies' against Panther leaders.

The Black Panthers and United Slaves were, in the California of the late sixties, rival contenders for the allegiance of black militants. The Panthers were much the larger and more political organisation, with a Marxist programme and a readiness to work with white Leftist groups. The smaller 'US' organisation described itself as 'cultural nationalist'. Its inspiration was Africa, it spurned any overt connection with whites and its politics were violently anti-communist, anti-Leftist and anti-Panther.

By 1968 the Panthers had become a major force in California's black ghettos. The consequent war waged on them by law enforcement agencies, stripping them of many of their leaders and militants, has become a matter of history. Hidden in that history is the extraordinary story of how the Los Angeles Police Department used Karenga's United Slaves against the politically more sophisticated (and to the establishment, more dangerous) organisation of Huey Newton and Bobby Seale.

According to Tackwood, his job for CCS on the Los Angeles Police Department's 'Black Desk' was to supply Karenga and United Slaves with the wherewithal to eliminate Panther leaders. At the end of 1968 there was a series of violent incidents involving the two groups and in January 1969 two Panther student leaders were shot dead. Three United Slaves' members were convicted of the murders; among the convicted were two brothers, Larry and George Stiner.

Tackwood later went public with the information that DeFreeze was one of the CCS agents recruited to work on the LAPD's 'Black Desk'; that the Stiner brothers were DeFreeze's contacts in the Karenga organisation; that DeFreeze's brief was to report on black militant activity in the South Central Los Angeles area, and that the cache of 200 guns found in Ronald Coleman's apartment was subsequently distributed to United Slaves by the police department, possibly through DeFreeze.

Tackwood's uncorroborated evidence is not conclusive proof that DeFreeze made the all-important move from informer to agent or *agent provocateur*. The word of an informer who informs on his fellow-informers is open to question. But earlier Tackwood revelations which at first were dismissed as fantasies later turned out to be unnervingly true. Moreover, his revelation of DeFreeze's assignment at this period only serves to add flesh to the bare bones of what is known from other sources of DeFreeze's police connections.

CCS agent and 'Black Desk' informer, DeFreeze nevertheless continued to get himself into trouble. On 16 August 1968 he was arrested and charged with grand larceny, but *again* got away with it. His wife, by whom he had now fathered three children to add to his three step-children, wrote to the police reminding them of DeFreeze's work for them and of the protection she claimed he had been promised. The charge was withdrawn. Again, in April the following year, DeFreeze was arrested for unlawful possession of a dangerous weapon, 'a military-type semi-automatic M-68 9mm rifle, fully loaded with an attached clip containing 32 bullets'. But he told the judge the gun was for a police officer friend, and once more escaped jail.

Next month DeFreeze appeared in Newark, New Jersey, the star figure in a strange incident which foreshadowed his later exploits. Posing as Black Panthers, DeFreeze and a partner held up a synagogue caretaker with a shotgun and tried to force the man to help them kidnap a well-known local Jewish leader. The idea, the caretaker later told the police, was that DeFreeze would demand a ransom by submitting to the press a communiqué which would purport to come from the Black Panther Party.

Since the caretaker wasn't very co-operative, DeFreeze settled for robbing him and made off across State lines to Cleveland, Ohio. There, on 11 October, he was arrested on the roof of the Cleveland Trust Company Bank and found to be in possession of a .38 revolver, a .25 calibre pistol, an eight inch dagger, a burglary kit and, in violation of federal law, a hand grenade. It was his eighth court appearance on firearms charges and he was wanted on a capital charge (conspiracy to kidnap) in New Jersey, not to mention probation violation in California. But Cleveland set him free on $5000 bail – and later dropped the charges.

On at least six occasions DeFreeze had serious charges against him quietly withdrawn. He must have been a valuable weapon in the LAPD's fight against criminal subversion. And with every instance that demonstrated his apparent immunity to the law, DeFreeze's sense of invincibility grew stronger.

When Cleveland freed him he again returned to Los Angeles, where he is said by Tackwood to have worked with detectives on the Manson case, allegedly planting arms on Manson's 'family'. But with the confidence that came from a conviction that the law no longer dared touch him, he was soon at his old tricks again, this time robbing a woman at gunpoint of a $1000 cheque. He tried to cash the cheque at a Los Angeles bank, shot and wounded a clerk who raised the alarm, and was arrested on 11 November. The gun he used was from the cache of 200 taken in the 1967 Coleman robbery. DeFreeze had contrived, or been allowed, to keep some of the proceeds of that haul.

At last, in 1970, the Los Angeles Police Department disowned him. Brought to trial, DeFreeze threatened to blow the gaff on police intelligence operations and tried to subpoena District Attorney Younger to appear in his defence. It was in vain. A report from the DA's office described him as 'a high-risk danger to society' who, if given his freedom, 'will return to his same violent career'. The report ventured the opinion that 'this defendant will eventually kill someone', since his actions indicated 'a total lack of regard for human life'.

DeFreeze was dispatched for an indefinite stay in the psychiatric facility at Vacaville. There he gave himself the African name Mtume and wrote long letters to his judges, one of which warned: 'You can smile and laugh at me and call me a fool for you think the Power of my Life is in your hands. But your power my God will take. For I am not alone.'

In 1971 Colston Westbrook took over the Black Cultural Association classes. DeFreeze became an enthusiastic participant. 'I

was a good listener and he likes to talk,' says Westbrook. 'I
don't know many people as sharp as DeFreeze – he has a lot of
savvy. He was a dedicated, high-driving brother, well respected.
He was charismatic and there was a certain faction behind him.'

Willie Wolfe and Russell Little were leading enthusiasts in
DeFreeze's faction, fascinated by the man's violent rhetoric and
defiant, compelling sense of style. He had abandoned the name
Mtume and given himself a 're-born' name, Cinque, borrowed
from an African chief who led a slave rebellion in the 1830s
and later, ironically, betrayed the cause of freedom by turning
slaver himself. DeFreeze pronounced the name 'Sink-you', or
just 'Sin'.

Cinque in turn must have been no less fascinated by the
white radicals – probably the first he had met – who came as
tutors and offered themselves as disciples. Within this mutual
admiration society the young whites expiated their guilt as
representatives of the white oppressors by sitting at the feet of
an oppressed black, a sharp dude who had never known anything but crime and the double-cross. DeFreeze began to
develop a political dimension, a larger framework for his
previously solitary rebellion.

Most of Cinque's faction were white outsiders. Despite Westbrook's testimonial he seems to have made enemies among his
fellow black inmates. And that was soon to split the BCA apart.
The split began with sex. In the free unsupervised sessions, some
of the visiting white girls had a direct and uninhibited way of
showing the prisoners someone loved them. While some got on
with the serious business of earnest revolutionary conversation,
others were making love under the wooden stage. Professor
Westbrook turned a blind eye to all this and even abetted the
therapy by bringing in black girls of his own. 'Sure I took some
foxes, some of my prime stock in there,' he was to admit later
to a *New York Times* reporter. 'Because if you want to dangle
a carrot in front of the inmates to get them to come to meetings,
you don't dangle communism. You dangle fine-looking chicks
they'll think maybe they can get to.'

What to the inmates was a happy choice of chocolate or
cream was to 'the lesbians of the SLA', as Westbrook later

called them, a strictly ideological matter. To offer their own
bodies to the black prisoners was a progressive gesture of anti-
racism and anti-sexism. To allow the same liberty to black
prostitutes was to connive at reactionary sexist exploitation. So
Westbrook came under increasingly bitter attack from the
radical elements he himself had introduced to the prison
meetings.

The dispute came to a head when the BCA held an election
for chairman in the autumn of 1972. The radicals backed
DeFreeze, not because he voiced an ideological aversion to
Westbrook's 'foxes' but because he had become their man.
However most of the inmates backed Westbrook's candidate,
and it was Westbrook's man who won, but to avert the collapse
of the BCA, Cinque was given charge of his own organisation
within the Association's umbrella. He called it Unisight, and it
included, of course, Wolfe, Little, the Berkeley radicals and one
additional black inmate, a short, thick-set, illiterate man named
Thero Wheeler.

Unisight was supposedly concerned with 'the study of the
problems of the black family'. In fact it studied and prepared
for an urban guerrilla insurrection using a method pioneered
by the Weathermen of 1969. The Weathermen had held 'gut-
check' struggle sessions to test a potential cadre's commitment,
asking 'Are you revolutionary enough to smash your closest
relationships? Are you revolutionary enough to give away your
children?' Unisight asked questions like: 'What would you do
if your mother was found to be a reactionary? Would you kill
her? Are bourgeois babies pigs? Would you kill them?'

The name 'Unisight', with its vague suggestion of racial or
political unity, was a clumsy foreshadowing of the more elegant
concept of symbiosis. This was most apparent in the group's
choice of a symbol: the seven-headed cobra. It was soon to be
known across the world as the sign of the SLA, but it had also
been used in the 1960s by Ron Karenga's United Slaves, making
for a fertile line of conspiracy theory. Was DeFreeze still involved, while inside Vacaville, with police-inspired 'cultural
nationalism' directed *against* the Left?

Two further events nourished this conspiracy theory. The

first was DeFreeze's sudden transfer in December from Vacaville to Soledad. Since Panther activity had been growing in
Soledad, following George Jackson's death and the Angela
Davis case, conspiracy theorists argued that DeFreeze was
perhaps transferred to inform on and entrap militants there.

The second event was DeFreeze's escape. Three months after
being transferred, on 5 March 1973, DeFreeze walked out of
Soledad. The jail is classified as maximum security, one of the
tightest of California's thirteen prisons. But on 5 March De-
Freeze was escorted from Central section, with its look-out
towers, armed guards and dog patrols, to the abandoned and
empty South section. South was due for renovation and De-
Freeze was taken that night to work on the boiler. Shortly after
midnight the one guard who was with him left him alone.
DeFreeze made off over the wall and was away.

These strange circumstances seem still stranger in the light of
evidence alleged to have been collected by private investigators
working for the group to which Louis Tackwood had defected
from the police, the Citizens Research and Investigation Committee. In May 1974 CRIC claimed that an unnamed Soledad
inmate had given them the following statement.

While Donald DeFreeze was here, I had a few conversations with him. I have always questioned his departure as
being a simple walk-away. I didn't come in contact with him
personally until his last couple of weeks here. There weren't
many who would associate with him. He tried to give the
impression of being super-cool and he came across as cold.
When I met him he was working in the maintenance shop. I
asked him if he was happy on his job, because if not, I might
be able to find him something else. He replied that within a
few days he was going to be assigned to work in the boiler
room at the South Facility. I questioned that because he
didn't have enough time here to be given that trust. I know
cons that have been turned down for that position. He
wouldn't comment; he only gave me a big smile. I should
explain that no prisoners were kept at the South Facility at
that time because it had no security. No gun towers were in

operation, and there were no guards posted. A few prisoners with proven records of trust were taken from Central Facility to the South Facility to perform certain duties: then they would be returned to Central after their shift. A few days later, DeFreeze did get that job: midnight to 8 am shift, in the boiler room at South Facility. On his first night he was dropped off at midnight, and given a few instructions. His job was automatic: it only required an overseer. Then he was left to himself and when an officer returned an hour later to check on him, he was gone.

CRIC used this statement to support a thesis that DeFreeze remained throughout a loyal police agent whose 'escape' was arranged by the authorities to put him back on his old job of discrediting militants and creating excuses for a general crack-down on the Left. All other elements of the story had to be dovetailed into the theory. So the Black Cultural Association became a front for a CIA-financed 'behaviour modification' programme designed to neutralise militants and, more specific-ally, to turn them against the Panthers. Colston Westbrook was labelled a CIA agent. DeFreeze was given free rein, first in the BCA itself and then in Unisight, to act as a magnet for white radicals, who would then be kept under surveillance. By creat-ing grotesque and deformed revolutionaries, the police could discredit 'real' revolutionaries. DeFreeze's escape was part of the plot, the SLA was part of the plot, even the kidnapping of Patty Hearst was part of the plot.

What must surely be the truth is rather more credible but no less dramatic than that. DeFreeze was certainly a police spy before he went to Vacaville and he may have had a residual connection with the police while in prison. But in the BCA, in Unisight and in the company of the white revolutionaries who both taught him and conferred dignity by learning from him, he found a new personality and purpose. He became, with all his deformations, at least a kind of revolutionary.

A police spy, not a rich heiress, was the SLA's first convert.

3   The Seven-Headed Cobra

In the dark early hours of 6 March 1973, Donald DeFreeze made his way from Soledad to Berkeley. Had his escape been connived at by the prison authorities or arranged by his colleagues in the LAPD Criminal Conspiracy Section, it is to Berkeley he would have gone to begin his mission of entrapment. Had he been sprung by his new revolutionary friends, it is to Berkeley he would have gone to join up with them. Had his walk-out been a simple, unaided escape, again it is to Berkeley he would have gone to seek the protection of the only friends he had in California.

His first protector was a girl named Amanda de Normanville, a former Berkeley student in the school of criminology and one of his BCA visitors who was said to have become romantically involved with him. Acquaintances described her as 'bubbling hot and sexy'. But DeFreeze stayed no more than a few hours in her apartment, anticipating (wrongly, as it happened) that police enquiries would quickly be made at the homes of all BCA-registered visitors, particularly those who had been closely associated with DeFreeze in Unisight. The group made hurried arrangements to transfer DeFreeze to a safe hideout.

So he moved in with Mizmoon, who had lately moved out of the apartment she had been sharing with Camilla Hall.

Although not on the BCA list herself, Mizmoon was dating Chris Thompson of the Chabot Road 'Peking House' commune. Thompson in turn was double-dating with Nancy Ling Perry. Some time in March, DeFreeze and Nancy met for the first time.

Nancy had been an ardent prison visitor for the past year but quite independently of the BCA. Captain Stanley Feaster, the Vacaville officer whose duty it was to vet BCA visitors with Professor Westbrook, ruled her out because she was already privately visiting three Vacaville inmates: 'Death Row' Jefferson, Albert Taylor and Raymond Sparks. Feaster apparently thought her unsuitable anyway. 'This is supposed to be an education, not a social experience,' he told her.

The impressionable Nancy, who was sleeping with Thompson and had started writing love letters to Albert Taylor, now fell for DeFreeze. She didn't take him from Mizmoon, but the two girls shared him. Despite the fact that DeFreeze was supposed to be in hiding, they made a bizarre and much-talked-of ménage-à-trois on Channing Way: tiny Nancy from the orange juice stand, the strident lesbian Mizmoon and big, black, bespectacled Donald DeFreeze, who called himself Cinque.

Nancy wrote a poem to her new lover. Police found the typescript months later, damaged by fire and incomplete in its closing lines.

> I love you
> I love you Sweet struggling man
> hear me without words
> totally surprised
> you came to me
> I came to you,
> Joined towards revolution.
>
> That I might see you
> after this struggle
> is well on its way
> and we can walk
> country roads

Knowing the Man has been offed
and we are all lovingly
building
lives
without fighting off a monster's
. . . death grip . . . all
. . . same time.
. . . the children's screams
. . . and cooed
. . . pleasure
. . . you, Sweet man
. . . work to do.

By the summer of 1973, DeFreeze, Nancy, Mizmoon, Camilla, Angela, Bill and Emily Harris, Willie Wolfe and Russell Little were meeting regularly as a revolutionary but not yet wholly clandestine group. Wolfe was active in Vietnam Veterans Against the War, the Harrises were involved on the fringes of the fast-disintegrating Venceremos Organisation which was racked both by ideological disputes over revolutionary violence and by police infiltration. Most were still caught up in the prison movement. Astonishingly, no official curb was placed either on the BCA or Unisight after DeFreeze's escape.

Some time in April or May, Willie Wolfe brought into the circle a fellow-member of Vietnam Veterans Against the War. Joseph Michael Remiro was from a white working-class family in San Francisco. He had served two voluntary hitches in Vietnam as a member of the 101st Airborne Division before his release in 1968. In 1970 he had achieved brief heroic stature with the radical underground by getting himself arrested for desecrating the American flag, which he had sewn on the seat of his pants. That won him a thirty-day suspended jail sentence which later disqualified him from joining his friends in registered prison visiting.

In 1972 Joseph Remiro became a founder-member of the East Bay chapter of VVAW, working in its office on Telegraph Avenue, Berkeley, where the telephone was installed and listed in his name. From the anti-war movement he moved on to more revolutionary activity with Venceremos and the Black Panthers. By March 1973, when Wolfe met him, he was abandoning VVAW as 'reformist and bourgeois-pacifist'. In July he walked into the Traders Gun Shop in San Leandro and taking full advantage of California's easy-going gun laws bought a .380 Walther pistol.

Later that month he started the Chabot Gun Club which provided cover for gun classes, a 'self-defence' course, and shooting practice in Wildcat Canyon, behind the Berkeley campus. Willie Wolfe, Russell Little and Emily Harris were among his students, acquiring second-hand the skills Remiro had learnt at Government expense in Vietnam.

Little also bought a gun of his own. Chris Thompson, the ex-boyfriend of both Nancy Ling Perry and Mizmoon, now supplanted by DeFreeze, was to testify to a Federal Grand Jury a few months later that he sold Little a .28 Rossi pistol. DeFreeze, while he seems to have had few or no contacts in the San Francisco area's black communities, must have known how to lay his hands on unregistered guns. A quantity of gun parts was collected together and fashioned into serviceable weapons by Remiro, a skilled and ingenious mechanic.

But the biggest single haul came from a series of well-planned burglaries. Late in July several radicals in the Bay Area had their houses and apartments broken into and their registered weapons stolen. The embryonic liberation army had decided that if self-proclaimed revolutionaries were never going to progress from talking revolution to making it, they didn't need guns. So Nancy Ling Perry put to a revolutionary purpose her gift for appropriating others' property. It was the group's first action.

That July Nancy also stopped taking drugs. She told Rudy Henderson she was giving them up because they impaired her political judgement. Henderson thought her politics naïve and a little dated. Four or five years after the rest of the student Left had got through its romantic trip with Che's Bolivians and the Tupumaros, Nancy and her friends, it seemed to him, were just discovering them.

By the end of the month the group had found a name which was soon to send policemen, politicians and newsmen scurrying first to their atlases and then to their dictionaries. It was surely Nancy, long-time student of the esoteric and now working part-time as a lab assistant, who rescued the word symbiosis from academic obscurity and turned it into a memorable metaphor for racial and sexual interdependence. As fungus and algae, shark and pilot fish, exist only in dependence on each other, so oppressed blacks and whites, men and women, could make the revolution only in symbiotic relationship with each other, united in the Symbionese Liberation Army.

If there were plenty of pilot fish, however, there was precious little shark. With Thompson's departure, DeFreeze was the only black in this inter-racial army. It is part of the mythology of the American Left that, given their objective condition as an oppressed substratum, the blacks must give the revolution its impetus and provide its leadership, so the SLA's Marxist credentials looked somewhat shaky. They could make amends to some extent by giving DeFreeze the nominal leadership, but it took more than one black leader to make a symbiosis.

The best recruiting ground was the prison system. Wolfe, Little, Nancy Ling Perry and the Harrises remained obsessive prison visitors. While much of their work was now being channelled through a more broadly based body called the United Prisoners Union, Wolfe and Little were still active in the BCA and Unisight at Vacaville.

The chairmanship of Unisight, since DeFreeze's escape, had fallen to a twenty-eight-year-old illiterate burglar named Thero Wheeler, known to his friends as 'The Gorilla'. Wheeler had been transferred to Vacaville from Soledad where he had been active in Venceremos and the United Prisoners Union. His transfer to the lower-security jail followed his sudden resignation from these organisations, and prompted a suspicion among some of his fellow inmates that Wheeler had done a deal with the prison authorities. These suspicions were heightened when, on 2 August, Wheeler was assigned to work cutting grass outside the prison walls, and made his escape.

The incident is curiously similar to DeFreeze's escape five

months earlier. Again, a prisoner with known radical connections outside – indeed, the very connections DeFreeze had –
was left virtually unsupervised in a position from which escape
was almost invited. And again, it seems, the police made no
enquiries of the visitors on the BCA register.

This is the stuff on which conspiracy theories thrive. Was
Wheeler too a police spy, sent on his way to infiltrate the SLA?
In a scenario where the incredible was soon to become common-
place, and where Wheeler's own part was to remain one of the
unsolved mysteries, it is not impossible. But the greater probability is that Wheeler, like hundreds of successful escapees
before him, simply took advantage of a security slip-up, seized
the moment, and bolted. Perhaps, as the FBI maintain, he had
outside help. However that may be, he arrived with the SLA at
the right moment to firm up the symbiosis by doubling its black
membership.

The SLA now needed to consolidate plans for securing a safe
hideaway from which to launch its impending onslaught on the
might of American capitalism. Nancy Ling Perry's address at
3856 Avenue, Oakland, had until now been the group's un-
official headquarters, but after Wheeler's escape it was again
thought unsafe to use any addresses on the prison visitors'
register. Little's address at 'Peking House' was widely known as
a radical hot-bed which would be sure to attract police attention
in time of trouble. Remiro's house in Bond Street, Oakland,
was 'clean', but he shared it with respectable parents who would
not have taken kindly to being moved out of the drawing-room
whenever the war council convened a meeting.

The sanctuary finally chosen by the group was a respectable,
middle-class house at 1560 Sutherland Court, a quiet cul-de-sac
in the Clayton Valley at Concord, 120 miles from Berkeley. One
advantage was that its owner lived in New York, an absentee
landlord. A deposit of $100 and a month's rent of $500 was paid
by money order on 14 August in the name of Nancy DeVoto,
and the couple who were to be known to neighbours as Nancy
and George DeVoto moved in the same week.

The DeVotos were Nancy Ling Perry and Russell Little.
Nancy had borrowed the name from an old schoolfriend who

was now the unsuspecting wife of a Santa Rosa art dealer. Other
SLA members also started to use aliases. Remiro called himself Scott Patterson and took out a temporary driver's licence
and a social security card in that name. Emily Harris used the
name Lynn Ledworth. Little, as well as calling himself DeVoto,
also used the alias Robert James Scalise, which later turned out
to be the name of a six-year-old Oakland boy who had died
twenty years earlier.

At 1560 Sutherland Court, enveloped in the security of their
developing fantasies, the SLA theoreticians began writing the
documents which they believed would release the latent revolutionary energies of the masses and strike at the vitals of Fascist
America. Like DeFreeze, they gave themselves 'reborn' names,
the origins of which seem to lie in Nancy's former cultish
enthusiasms. She herself became 'Fahizah', Camilla 'Gabi',
Mizmoon 'Zoya', Angela 'Gelina', Emily 'Yolande', Willie
Wolfe 'Cujo', Bill Harris 'Tico', Russell Little 'Osceola' and Joe
Remiro 'Bo'.

Their first public document was a leaflet run off on one of the
hundreds of offset-litho machines to be found in basements all
over Berkeley. It featured the striking and menacing symbol
which only a few months later would be known around the
world as the SLA's war emblem: the seven-headed cobra. The
SLA did not invent it. To the ancient Egyptians and in Hindu
mythology the device represented both indestructibility and a
mystical unity in diversity. Nancy may have discovered it during
her 'Egyptian period', though it had already begun to enjoy
something of a revival on the esoteric fringes of Californian
'sixties culture'. Jimi Hendrix used it as a sleeve decoration
on one of his record albums in 1967. More pointedly, Karenga's
United Slaves had chosen it as the symbol of African 'cultural
nationalism'. DeFreeze would certainly have known of it from
his own police-contact work with 'US', which suggests it was he
rather than Nancy who appropriated it for the SLA. Indeed,
there is a story in Berkeley that DeFreeze, whose carelessness in
matters of security was later to cost the SLA dear, himself used
the Berkeley public library Xerox machine to copy the symbol
from the Egyptian *Book of the Dead*, and walked out leaving

the original lying in full view on the machine. His own sense of invulnerability must have been as powerful as the cobra's.

The text of the SLA's leaflet, beneath the symbol, set out to explain the 'unity-in-diversity' concept of symbiosis, directed towards the 'common goal of freedom from the chains of capitalism':

The seven memberships of our federation are men and women who are black, brown, yellow, red, white, young and old . . .

Each member lives and speaks and fights for the best interests of all within the body, just as no one head of the cobra can be attacked without the others rising to strike with venom in self defense to destroy the attacker . . .

The SLA will build and fight for the socialist unity of all oppressed peoples. A cry from any one of us will echo in the body of our common ear and we will attack out of instinct and in self defense for our survival.

The message ended with the slogan that was to sign off the SLA's future communiqués: 'With the venom of our seven heads we will destroy the fascist insect who preys upon the life of the people.'

The 'seven principles' were spelt out under headlines in three languages: Swahili, which some black cultural nationalists expected to become the 'true' language of black America; Spanish, spoken by California's huge population of Mexican migrants and Chicanos; and finally, English.

UMOHA – LAS UNIDAD – UNITY: To strive for and maintain unity in our household, our nation and in The Symbionese Federation.

KUJICHAGULIA – LA LIBRE DETERMINACION – SELF DETERMINATION: To define ourselves, name ourselves, speak for ourselves and govern ourselves.

UJIMA – TRABAJO COLECTIVO Y RESPONSI- BILIDAD – COLLECTIVE WORK AND RESPONSI- BILITY: To build and maintain our nation and the federation together by making our brothers' and sisters' and the Federation's problems our problems and solving them together.

UJAMAA – PRODUCCION COOPERATIVA – CO-OPERATIVE PRODUCTION: To build and maintain our own economy from our skills and labor and resources and to ensure ourselves and other nations that we all profit equally from our labor.

NIA – PROPOSITO – PURPOSE: To make as our collective vocation the development and liberation of our nation, and all oppressed people, in order to restore our people and all oppressed people to their traditional greatness and humanity.

KUUMBA – CREATIVO – CREATIVITY: To do all we can, as best we can, in order to free our nation and defend the federation and constantly make it and the earth we all share more beautiful and beneficial.

IMANI – FE – FAITH: To believe in our unity, our leaders, our teachers, our people and in the righteousness and victory of our struggle and the struggle of all oppressed and exploited people.

To those who would hear the hopes and future of our people, let the voice of their guns express the words of freedom.

The emphasis on 'nation' and 'the federation' was continued in a second document which set out 'The Goals of the Symbionese Liberation Army'. Borrowing concepts and terminology from the black cultural nationalist movement, the SLA identified the masses not in Marxist or socialist terms of class, defined in relation to capital and labour, but in terms of nation and race. But where the black cultural nationalists had set out to create a black nation within America, the SLA envisaged a series of 'sovereign nations' representing the blacks, browns, yellows, reds and whites. This 'system of sovereign nations that are in the total interest of all its races and people' would be built on the ashes of 'the capitalist state and all its value systems', once capitalism had been destroyed by 'all oppressed people' united in 'a fighting force'. Within these 'nations', said the SLA, the

people would have the right to 'select and elect their own
representatives and governments by direct vote', and each
nation would be represented on a 'people's federated council,
the Symbionese Federation of Nations', by 'a male and a female
of each People's Council or Sovereign Nation'.

Woven into this extraordinary amalgam of Nancy's dreams
and DeFreeze's confusions was a saner thread of more orthodox
socialism, perhaps contributed by the Harrises. The SLA, said
the leaflet, 'aimed to place the control of all the institutions
and industries of each nation into the hands of its people . . .
To take control of all state land and that of the capitalist class
and to give back the land to the people . . . No-one can own or
sell the air, the sky, the water, the trees, the birds, the sun, for
all of this world belongs to the people of this earth.' The SLA
would 'take control of all buildings and apartment buildings
of the capitalist class and fascist government and totally destroy
the rent system of exploitation.' Industry would be run 'not for
profit but in the full interest of all the people' and the SLA
would 'destroy all forms and institutions of Racism, Sexism,
Ageism, Capitalism, Fascism, Individualism, Possessiveness,
Competitiveness and all other such institutions that have made
and sustained capitalism and the capitalist class system that has
oppressed and exploited all of the people of our history.'

There were also goals which reflected the liberal and
humanitarian concerns of the Berkeley community: 'To create
a system where our aged are cared for with respect, love and
kindness . . . To create a system and laws that will neither force
people into nor force them to stay in personal relationships that
they do not wish to be in . . . To form communes on the community level', bringing children into 'the care and loving interest
of the revolutionary community'. Further, the prison system,
'which the capitalist state has used to imprison the oppressed and
exploited, and thereby destroy the love, unity and hopes of
millions of lives and families' would be replaced by 'a system
of comradeship and group unity and education on a communal
and revolutionary level'.

Finally, in what was probably a contribution from Mizmoon
and Camilla, the SLA aimed 'to create institutions that will aid,

reinforce and educate the growth of our comrade women and aid them in making a new, true and better role to live in life and in the defining of themselves as a new and free people'.

The 'Goals' document bears all the marks of collective drafting. The SLA's third document, described as a 'Symbionese Programme', attempted to draw the threads together and was probably written by Mizmoon and DeFreeze. It described 'the Symbionese Federation and the Symbionese Liberation Army' in typically grandiose terms as 'a united and federated grouping of members of different races and people and socialist political parties of the oppressed people of the Fascist United States of America'. It had been formed 'under black and minority leadership' to 'struggle in a united front for the independance [sic] and self-determination of each of their races and people and The Liquidation of the Common Enemy. The document went on:

> The Symbionese Liberation Army is an army of the people, and is made up of members of all the people.
> The SLA has no political power or political person over it that dictates who will fight and die if needed for the freedom of our people and children, but does not risk their life or fight too for our freedom, but rather the SLA is both political and military in that in the SLA the army officer, whether female or male, is also the political officer and they both are the daughters and sons of the people and they both fight as well as speak for the freedom of our people and children . . .
> The name Symbionese is taken from the word symbiosis and we define its meaning as a body of dissimilar bodies and organisms living in deep and loving harmony and partnership in the best interests of all within the body.
> We define ourselves by this name because it states that we are no longer willing to allow the enemy of all our people and children to murder, oppress and exploit us, nor define us by color and thereby maintain division among us, but rather have we joined together . . . to build a better and new world for our children and people's future. We are a United Front and Federated Coalition of members from the Asian,

Black, Brown, Indian, White, Women, Grey [ie old] and Gay
Liberation Movements who have all come to see and understand that only if we unite and build our new world and
future, will there really be a future for our children and
people. We of the People, and not the ruling capitalist class,
will build a new world and system where there is really
freedom and a true meaning to justice and equality for all
women and men of all races and people, and an end to the
murder and oppression, exploitation of all people.

We of the Symbionese Federation and the SLA . . . have
decided to redefine ourselves as a Symbionese Race and
People . . . We are now able to become a united people under
the Symbionese Federation and make true the words of our
codes of unity that TO DIE A RACE AND BE BORN A
NATION IS TO BECOME FREE.

There followed the SLA's public 'Declaration of Revolutionary War':

Therefore we of the Symbionese Federation and the SLA
DO NOT under the rights of human beings submit to the
murder, oppression and exploitation of our children and
people, and *DO* under the rights granted to the people under
The Declaration of Independance [sic] of the United States,
do now by the rights of our children and people and by Force
of Arms and with every drop of our blood, DECLARE
REVOLUTIONARY WAR against The Fascist Capitalist
Class and all their agents of murder, oppression and exploitation. We support by Force of Arms the just struggles of all
oppressed people for self determination and independance
[sic] within the United States and The World. And hereby
offer to all liberation movements, revolutionary workers'
groups, and people's organisations our total aid and support
for the struggle for freedom and justice for all people and
races. We call upon all revolutionary black and other
oppressed people within the Fascist United States to come
together to join The Symbionese Federation and fight in the
forces of The Symbionese Liberation Army.

The 'Goals', 'Programme' and 'Declaration of Revolutionary

War' clarify not what the SLA *was* but how its handful of
members saw themselves. The breadth of support of which they
boasted was no more than an aspiration. There was no 'United
Front', no 'Federated Coalition', no Asian, Brown, Indian or
'Grey' support. There was scarcely yet an army. The SLA was,
in fact, two black convicts and a handful of white students:
eleven apprentice disciples of the gospel of revolution.

On 21 August they sent their confused, misspelt tracts and
their 'Declaration of Revolutionary War' to the San Francisco
newspapers, radio and television. Then they waited expectantly
for the first signs of the alarm and terror that must surely grip
the enemies of the people as they heard the unmistakable
rumbling of the tumbrils.

In a dozen newsrooms the duty sub, long accustomed to a
daily flow of eccentric missives from assorted nuts, gurus,
pranksters and self-appointed field-marshals, tossed the SLA's
communiqué into the waste-bin. The revolution had begun –
and no one noticed.

The SLA had described itself as a coalition of socialist parties,
and had boasted of offering its armed services to all liberation
movements, revolutionary groups and peoples' organisations.
The organisations to which it made specific approaches during
the summer of 1973 were Venceremos, the Black Guerrilla
Family, the 'Polar Bear' Party, the United Prisoners Union and
the Oakland Coalition to Save Our Schools.

Several of the SLA had worked with members of Venceremos,
though only Thero Wheeler had actually belonged to it.
Venceremos had begun in the San Francisco peninsula as
a movement for solidarity with Cuba – hence its Spanish name.
By 1971 its politics had become broadly Maoist. In 1972 several
members were convicted of helping organise the escape of a
convict from Chino prison during which a guard was killed.
This case led to the formation of Chino Defense Committees, in
one of which Emily Harris and Angela Atwood were active.
By the summer of 1973, when the SLA was in the process of
coming together in Berkeley, the remnants of Venceremos,

ravaged by factional disputes and police harassment, were debating the pros and cons of an active guerrilla strategy, and when the leadership opposed it as self-defeating and 'ultra-Leftist', the movement split.

The SLA made a deliberate, planned attempt to recruit the pro-guerrilla faction but were turned down. Better versed in Marxist theory than the SLA, the Venceremos activists must have found the notion of a symbiotic federation of nations at best weird, at worst reactionary. Some of them instead formed their own organisation, the August Seventh Guerrilla Movement, which the SLA, no doubt in pique, was later to denounce as a police conspiracy – a common enough epithet on the fringe-Left for rival organisations.

After their rejection by Venceremos dissidents, the SLA turned to the Black Guerrilla Family, the political wing of the Black Liberation Army which had broken away from the Black Panther Party to follow Eldridge Cleaver. Cleaver had fallen out with Huey Newton and Bobby Seale when they began shifting the Panthers' emphasis from armed struggle to a 'consciousness-raising' programme of community politics. When Cleaver himself fled the country his faction retained strength only where his personal influence had been strong, making little headway in California except in the jails. The Harrises made a point of visiting Guerrilla Family prisoners, including the titular leader in California, 'Doc' Holiday, but while the Family was sympathetic to the SLA and probably helped later with sanctuary and supplies when the SLA was on the run, it avoided a formal tie-up, probably because it distrusted DeFreeze.

The 'Polar Bear' Party was perhaps the strangest of all the organisations courted by the SLA. It originated as a white-racist prison group committed to neo-Nazi notions of Aryan purity, probably in reaction against the growing political supremacy of black prisoners. The party described itself as 'a politically oriented group . . . to promote prison reform and fight for the abandonment of prison entirely'. By the end of 1972 it had so far departed from white racism as to join an alliance with mixed racial groups campaigning for reform, even including the avowedly revolutionary Venceremos organisation. Its members were surely the world's only white-racist Maoists and their incorporation into the Symbionese Federation would have tested the concept of symbiosis to its limit. Nancy Ling Perry was the regular visitor of at least one 'Polar Bear' member, Albert Taylor. But although she wrote him love letters she failed to persuade the Party to join the Symbionese Federation.

That left the United Prisoners Union. This was an organisation of inmates, parolees and ex-convicts dedicated to building a revolutionary prisoner class inside and around the Californian jail system. Nancy, Little and Wolfe were all active in its work and, according to some of its members, Nancy worked particularly hard on a committee member named Jessica Vodquen. It was fortunate for the SLA that Nancy again failed to make a convert because later in the year, when UPU chairman Wilber 'Popeye' Jackson was acquitted on a drugs charge, Jessica Vodquen was exposed by the defence at his trial as a police infiltrator.

Each of these groups was invited to join the Federation and send representatives to the 'United Symbionese War Council'. A schedule of 'Terms of Military/Political Alliance' was drawn up. Constituent bodies were required to prove that they would 'fight as well as talk' by presenting evidence that a 'combat action' had been carried out in the previous twelve months. Once accepted, they would have the right to 'select two persons, one female and one male (if possible)' for service on the War Council. Factions of organisations were acceptable as representatives of the whole organisation. They were expected to bring with them supplies of 'military equipment, materials, finances, and personnel'. Any 'restraining of supplies . . . for political reason or reactionary reasons or political chess games with the enemy' was 'punishable by death'.

Since the SLA had so much to demand and so little to offer, it is hardly surprising that its Federation never got off the ground. And in an atmosphere among all Leftist groups of paranoia over police infiltration and provocation, the proposed Federation looked uncomfortably like FBI or city police bait.

So, when the SLA went to war, it went alone.

*

In search of a popular, community-based cause to justify their first combat action, the tiny band of Berkeley revolutionaries found it in neighbouring Oakland.

All year a dispute had been simmering in the neighbourhood schools over what should be done to fight growing playground violence and drug abuse. The school administrators were for armed police patrols on school premises. Teachers wanted to carry arms themselves. Parents wanted to form their own patrols. The job of finding a workable compromise belonged to Dr Marcus Foster, the city's Superintendent of Schools, and his assistant, Robert Blackburn.

Foster was black. His appointment two years earlier was something of a victory for black and white-liberal pressure groups which had been campaigning to force the city to give more senior adminstrative jobs to qualified blacks. Foster was well-qualified: he came to Oakland from Philadelphia where he had won an award for his work among child drug addicts.

Hunting around for a course of action which would cut down on violence without offending any of the parties which were plying him with partisan advice, Foster had the bright idea of consulting the one party which no one had so far thought to consult: the children. At each school in turn he was assured that the knifings and dope-peddling were the fault of other children from other schools. 'All right,' said Foster, 'we'll give you all identity cards to isolate the outsiders.'

The plan seemed innocent enough, but it didn't go down at all well with Concerned Parents to Save our Schools, a mainly black parent body which had been campaigning for smaller classes, better teachers and bigger budgets and which now took up the fight against identity cards. Concerned Parents described the plan as 'smacking of South Africa's pass laws' and demanded to know why middle-class children in predominantly white schools were not to be subjected to the same 'indignity'.

The cause was taken up by assorted radical groups and Concerned Parents grew into the Coalition to Save our Schools, recruiting many non-parents. Among those who joined was Willie Wolfe.

Some time around June or July 1973, Wolfe took Coalition

'Co-Chairperson' Vera Silverman into Vacaville under the auspices of the ever-obliging BCA. Colston Westbrook remembers that 'she made a very tough speech against Foster and said some very inflammatory things'. In the heated discussion that followed, Foster was condemned as a 'white nigger' and an Uncle Tom. 'The white nigger has got his foot on your neck and now he's going to do the same thing to your children', said one black prisoner.

George Jackson had written in *Blood in My Eye* of 'the black pig who must learn that the reward for counter-revolution is death'. That summer in Vacaville Dr Marcus Foster was condemned as a black pig, a counter-revolutionary.

The SLA decided to kill Foster. They were convinced that their action would prove the superiority of gun-power over protest and swing the Left behind their leadership.

So Emily Harris, using the alias Lynn Redworth, took a three-month lease on a third-storey apartment at 1621 Seventh Avenue, five blocks and half a mile away from the school administration building where Foster had his office. Neighbours later identified Remiro and Little as regular visitors to the apartment. One neighbour remembers that the newcomers worked late into the night, apparently drilling holes for what seemed to be an impressive number of fixtures and fittings. Cartons of bullets were later found with their tips drilled ready for the insertion of a compound of cyanide.

The SLA may have used the Seventh Avenue apartment as a base from which to keep Foster under observation and as a sanctuary after the crime. But however thorough their preparations for the killing, they didn't go to much trouble to keep abreast of developments in the school's row. They even confused Marcus Foster with another education department official named Richard Foster, which nearly resulted in their killing the wrong man. Crucially, they failed to become aware of a decisive turning point in the Coalition's campaign.

At a meeting on 9 October Foster dropped the identity card plan. Perhaps influenced by a 2000-signature petition, but anxious anyway to defuse a dispute which had turned decidedly ugly, he simply refrained from putting the proposal on the agenda. So the matter was quietly dropped, without public announcement. The Coalition activists were made aware of Foster's retreat, and by the end of the month the news was around the community. But – understandably, since few knew of its existence and none knew of its plans – no one told the SLA.

On the night of Tuesday 6 November, Foster and his white deputy, Robert Blackburn, left the schools administration building by the back door after attending a late committee meeting. As they crossed the yard to their cars Blackburn noticed in the gathering darkness the outline of two people leaning against the wall. He decided they were stragglers from the meeting that had just ended, hoping, perhaps, for a lift.

Blackburn continued across the yard with Foster. Suddenly a succession of shots blasted out. Blackburn remembers an impression of muzzle flashes from two guns being fired almost simultaneously. Foster stumbled and fell forward on his face. Then Blackburn himself was hit and fell beside his chief. One of the gunmen ran forward and put six more shots in Foster's body. A duplicating supervisor who was working late ran into the yard and found Foster dead and Blackburn badly wounded. Witnesses told the police they saw three people running away. Each appeared to be wearing a shoulder-length wig, woollen denim jacket and dark jeans. All had their faces covered. Some witnesses were sure the killers were black men, accompanied perhaps by a white woman.

Two days later, the *Oakland Tribune*, *San Francisco Chronicle* and KPFA radio station received identical copies of a communiqué from the SLA. They were dated 6 November, the day of the killing, and police noted the irrelevant but ironic fact that they were mailed in envelopes bearing a Revolutionary War Bicentennial Commemorative stamp with the slogan 'Rise the Spirit of Independence'. With the communiqué was a copy of the seven-headed cobra leaflet.

It purported to come from the 'Western Regional Youth Unit of the SLA'. The communiqué said that a 'Court of the People' had found Foster and Blackburn 'guilty of supporting and taking part in crimes committed against the children and the life of the people'. Specifically, it accused them of plotting to foist identity cards on school children and introducing 'political police' into the schools. Foster, it said, was a 'Nixon police agent', a 'white nigger' assisting in 'genocide against blacks'. The letter served notice on 'the enemy police state and its lackeys' that it was the SLA's intention to shoot on sight other members of the education board who persisted in ignoring the wishes of the people.

This time the press did take notice and, for the first time, the public learned of the existence of the SLA. The *Chronicle* ran the letter, but reported that police were inclined to dismiss it as a hoax. The *Oakland Tribune* treated it seriously enough to call in the services of an expert in semantics, Dr S. I. Hayakawa, who surprisingly analysed the letter as the work of a 'high-grade intellect'. The doctor ventured the opinion that the author was 'devoted to revolutionary ideology' and guessed that the SLA believed in 'the kind of destruction aimed toward society by the SDS and the Weathermen'. But Dr Hayakawa solved one puzzle that had baffled police investigators. The references to 'Black, Chicano, Asian and conscious White Youth', he suggested, helped explain the use of the mystery word symbionese, which meant 'the partnership of dissimilar groups for their mutual benefit'.

What convinced the police and FBI that they were dealing with a real organisation, genuinely involved in the shooting, was a reference in the communiqué to the use of cyanide-tipped bullets. The coroner confirmed that the bullets recovered from Foster and Blackburn had indeed been drilled out at the tips and filled with a chemical mixture containing cyanide: not enough to kill, but enough to validate the SLA's claims and put a distinctively venomous seal on the actions of those who served under the banner of the cobra.

On 15 November the Oakland schools board publicly confirmed that no decision had been taken on an identity card system, adding that none would be 'until the feelings of students and parents can be reassessed'. This prompted a second SLA communiqué. Since 'the fascist Board of Education has made an attempt to heed and respect the rights and wishes of the people', it stated, the 'shoot on sight warrant' would be rescinded and 'all forces of the SLA and the Peoples Army [would] halt their attack on this aspect of the fascist enemy state'. But if the programme were reinstated, then 'the Death Warrant Order is to be immediately reactivated without warning'.

This second communiqué went on to query whether Blackburn (described as 'a CIA agent') had really survived the attack, as reported by the press, since 'traditionally the fascist news media is quick to display photographs of the enemy . . . as he lays in his plush, private hospital room, while the wounds of all oppressed people remain unattended'. But if he *was* alive, said the communiqué, the SLA was content to 'point out the contradiction between the medical care received by those who represent the ruling class, and that received by members of the poor and oppressed communities'.

It was a crude attempt to rally radical support, and in similar vein the communiqué went on to praise 'the spirit, determination and strength of the vast Black, Chicano, Asian and conscious white communities of the Oakland–Berkeley area' who would 'always understand the effectiveness and tactics of revolutionary justice'. The truth was, however, that Berkeley and Oakland communities were horrified by the killing and baffled that it was done by a movement claiming to belong to and speak for the Left. Their bewilderment turned to fury as the murder hunt was made an occasion for persistent police questioning and harassment of anyone in the community who had ever been active in any Left-wing or radical cause.

One of the fiercest attacks from the Left on the 'infantile adventurism' of the SLA was made by Black Panther leader, Huey Newton, who saw in the SLA a rebirth of Eldridge Cleaver's adventurist heresies. Newton's scathing denunciation was to result in his being put on the SLA's death list as a 'traitor to the people', and this in turn suggested to the Panthers that the SLA was a put-up job by the police – Karenga's United Slaves all over again.

For each member of the SLA the killing of Marcus Foster was the point of no return, the watershed between revolutionary intent and revolutionary action. For Nancy Ling Perry, who was almost certainly one of the three who fired the cyanide bullets into Foster's body, the killing seems to have been an act of personal liberation, the final proof, perhaps, to herself as much as to the outside world, that the Goldwater supporter, the high school cheerleader, was dead and reborn as Fahizah. And to Mizmoon, Camilla, Angela? They had not pulled the trigger nor seen Foster fall, but they had discussed, planned, assented to the elimination of this 'enemy of the people'. There was no going back now. In the weeks that followed, those of the group who had not already done so began to cut off their ties with the outside world.

Nancy Ling Perry wrote to her parents in December, ending: 'I wish love and happiness to everyone. Stay well, and well-informed. I love you, Nancy.' They never saw or heard from her again.

Mizmoon wrote to her parents saying she had 'work to do' and asking them to destroy all family photographs of her. They didn't do so, but that was the last they were ever to hear from her.

In January, Emily Harris wrote to her father and the letter revealed something of the shifting personal relationships within the SLA:

> I have learned a lot from Bill, from other people here in Oakland, and from the people in prison and they, in turn, have learned a lot from me. One person in particular – a beautiful black man – has conveyed to me the torture of being black in this country and of being poor. He has dedicated his life to eliminating the conditions that oppose people being able to lead satisfying lives and to replace these with conditions that make people truly free – so part of this process is to destroy and part is to rebuild . . . Bill and I have changed our relationship so that it no longer confines us and I am enjoying relationships with other men. I am in love with the black man I referred to earlier and that love is very beautiful and fulfilling.

Despite the questioning and cross-questioning of everyone involved in the Coalition to Save our Schools, the police found few leads in their search for Foster's killers. But twice their path crossed that of the SLA without their realising it. Once, checking out a van which had been seen near the scene of the killing, they questioned the owner, Gary Ling, who was Nancy's brother. Nancy may have used the van that night, but the police enquiry seems to have come to nothing. Then a day or two after questioning Gary Ling, the police not only questioned Nancy herself but actually did so on the doorstep of the SLA hide-away house in Concord. They were called there by neighbours after a curious incident in which a boy of about sixteen knocked on the door and spoke to Nancy, asking for 'George DeVoto'. When Nancy asked his name the boy pulled a gun on her. An argument broke out and the boy fired several shots before racing away on a motorcycle. Neighbours called the police who took a statement from Nancy, but since she signed it DeVoto there was no reason for them to connect her with the Gary Ling they had questioned earlier, and therefore no reason to link her to the SLA. So they left 1560 Sutherland Court without having any notion that they had been at the operational head-quarters of the new terrorist organisation everyone was reading about in the papers. But the incident – which remains un-explained – must have been something of a shock to those who were inside the house that weekend.

It was probably after this security lapse that preparations were made for a sudden siege. Doors and windows were re-inforced with plywood, and bales of newspapers were strung together as bullet-proof barricades. Under the floorboards, a tunnel was begun but abandoned. Gas masks were kept under the beds. But the police didn't return.

By Christmas, both the Foster killing and the SLA had been out of the news for a month. And in the Sierra Nevada, Patty Hearst and Steven Weed told the Hearsts they planned to marry next June.

The SLA had already made plans for its second combat action. But those plans were about to be interrupted.

*

The morning of 10 January 1974 was just one hour and twenty minutes old when Deputy Sheriff Sgt David Duge, patrolling in the Clayton Valley, Concord, in his unmarked patrol car, spotted what he was to describe in his notebook as a 'suspicious incident'. Most house lights were out and the neighbourhood was quiet. This was prime time and a prime locality for burglars. So the Deputy Sheriff wanted to know what that red Chevrolet van was doing at this time of night, driving very, very slowly and keeping close to the kerbside in Sutherland Drive.

He made a routine radio call to ask the station duty officer to check out the registration number – 806 GUD. He was told it was listed in the name of Perry at 3856 Whittle Avenue, Oakland. That was twenty miles away. So what was it doing here at 1.20 in the morning?

Sgt Duge switched off his lights, did a U-turn and followed the van at its own crawling pace. It turned left, then left again, then left a third time, until it was back at the intersection of Ayers Road and Sutherland Drive. Sgt Duge switched on his lights and pulled up in front of the van. There were two men inside. He walked round to the driver and asked him to identify himself. Russell Little gave the name Robert James Scalise and the address 1621 Seventh Street, Oakland. The policeman asked where they were headed. A well-trained urban guerrilla would have had a ready alibi. Little said 'the DeVoto residence'.

Sgt Duge turned back to his car to radio the station for the name of DeVoto to be checked on the central register. As he did so, either Little or his passenger, Joseph Remiro, pulled a gun on him and opened fire.

The shots missed Duge but shattered the windscreen of his patrol car. The policeman pulled his own gun and fired at the van, which was already trying for a quick getaway. One shot hit Little in the shoulder, another burst a tyre. The van stopped.

Remiro ran off on foot but Sgt Duge quickly overpowered Little and disarmed him of a .38 Colt revolver. Then he put out a call for help on his car radio. More patrol cars arrived, sirens wailing, and Little was bundled away. The Chevrolet was searched and police found one 9mm rifle – and 2000 SLA leaflets.

It is not clear what Little and Remiro were doing that night in Nancy Ling Perry's van. Since Little was living at 'the DeVoto residence', which was less than a hundred yards from the point where the van was stopped, they could hardly have been searching for it. Perhaps they were looking for someone who hadn't turned up and who they thought might be wandering lost in the streets. But why take SLA leaflets with them? And a rifle and two pistols?

The occupants of the 'DeVoto' house must have heard the shooting. They may have come running out with the other residents who poured into the street once the police arrived and were seen to be in control. Certainly it wasn't long before they knew that Little and Remiro would not be rejoining them.

Remiro evaded capture for nearly five hours before being found under a parked car in a yard near Sutherland Drive. He was armed with a .380 Walther semi-automatic pistol, but offered no resistance. Police ballistics experts were later to claim that the guns found on Remiro and Little that night were those that had killed Foster and wounded Blackburn two months earlier. The two were charged with murder and quickly transferred from the local jail to San Quentin.

As dawn broke on 10 January the police suddenly seemed all set to break the SLA. A general enquiry among neighbours was all that was needed to locate the 'DeVoto' house, which, in any case, the police should have known about from the 11 November shooting incident. And it didn't need much detective work to find the second hideout near the site of the Foster killing. Little had given the address 1621 Seventh *Street* which, when checked, proved to be a vacant parking lot, but it needed only one bright detective to think of trying 1621 Seventh *Avenue* and the SLA's second 'liberated zone' would have been rumbled. As it happened, the Concord police never thought to look for the 'DeVoto' house, and took a week to make the connection with Seventh Avenue. The SLA, though widely scattered, were quicker off the mark.

Emily Harris was working as a clerk-typist at the Survey Research Centre in Berkeley. Bill Harris was working as a temporary postman. Neither showed up for work on 10

January. Their apartment was later found empty, apparently abandoned at short notice. A pot of drip-through coffee was still standing on the stove.

San Quentin prison records show that on 10 January Emily visited a prisoner named Barron Broadnax of the Black Guerrilla Family. She didn't stay long. It was her last prison visit before she disappeared.

Angela Atwood failed to report that day for work at her job as a temporary waitress. She too visited a Black Guerrilla Family prisoner, 'Doc' Holiday, in San Quentin. She used the name Ann Lindberg, and again, it was her last visit.

Willie Wolfe was paying his family a visit in Philadelphia. On the morning of 11 January he took a long-distance call from the Bay Area. He told his mother he had to leave for New York immediately. His parents never saw or heard from him again.

Mizmoon had already abandoned her bungalow on Parker Street, Berkeley, for an unknown address. Camilla Hall, who had left Channing Way for a small house on Francisco Street, was the last to go to ground. She went suddenly on 19 February, leaving behind her beloved collection of old furniture and photographs and taking only her clothes and her siamese cat.

In their Sutherland Court hideout in the hours following the arrest of Little and Remiro, those members of the SLA who were in residence that night knew they were faced with the prospect of imminent discovery. Yet they seem to have been slow in organising their get-away. Nancy's van was now in police hands, but late in the afternoon someone brought round Willie Wolfe's battered Buick Riviera. Guns and ammunition were loaded into it and at 6.20 pm neighbours saw Nancy and three passengers making off at speed. The neighbours simultaneously saw smoke drifting out from under the front door of the house. Within minutes the Concord Fire Department was on the scene.

Petrol from a five-gallon drum had been splashed on walls and floors, but the firemen doused the flames before they could get a real hold. The result was that much of the greater part of the evidence of SLA occupancy was untouched by the fire. Nancy had bungled her first attempt at arson.

The police, who followed hard on the heels of the firemen, had a rich haul. They listed among their finds bottles and test tubes of various chemicals including potassium cyanide, bullets with the tips drilled and packed with cyanide, home-made pipe bombs and explosive powder, ammunition cartons for 12-gauge shotguns and .308 rifles, boxes of 9 mm ammunition and scores of parts from dismantled weapons. There was evidence that the SLA had made preparations for hiding out in the hills or deep in the city. There were walkie-talkie sets, maps marked with possible hideouts and escape routes, and plans of the Bay Area underground rail system, then under construction. Ironically, the very plans apparently prepared for an emergency flight were left behind when the emergency materialised.

The police took away a stack of revolutionary and Women's Lib posters but left dozens of books, many of them stolen from the Berkeley public library. They included a history of the Soviet Communist Party and two works by Brazilian urban guerrilla leader Carlos Marighella, killed in a police ambush in 1969: *The Manual of Guerrilla Warfare* and *For the Liberation*. In the margins were scrawled such comments as 'Fuck the upper and supposed middle class!'; 'The oppressed will eat and be free', and 'The oppressors will change or die by our guns'.

Police also found a 'hit list' of 'enemies of the people' marked down for 'execution'. They included bankers, business-men and, incongruously, Huey Newton of the Black Panthers who had denounced the SLA after the Foster killing. There was also evidence of a plan for a mass breakout from Vacaville, coupled with the outline of a plot for assassinating selected prison officials. A floor plan of the Berkeley Post Office – where Bill Harris was currently working as a temporary postman – marked the positions of the safes, suggesting one source from which the SLA proposed to finance its operations. There was also one harmless item, a set of hair grooming aids of a type used by black people, confirming the presence of blacks in the SLA.

The Concord police gave the haul – particularly the weapons – massive publicity, keen that the world should understand what a nest of cobras they had uncovered. Yet there were finds they failed to publicise. One was a library card in the name of Gary

Atwood, Angela's estranged husband. Properly followed up, this might have proved a potent lead – but the police ignored it. They also ignored a much more important find, a piece of paper with a handwritten scrawl which might have been torn from a notebook or could alternatively have been the draft of a communiqué. It outlined a plan to 'expose the international crimes of B of A' – presumably the Bank of America – and continued with the cryptic phrases: 'Patricia Hearst, on the night of the full moon, January 7 . . . junior art student . . . daughter of Hearst'. The scrawl continued with references to an apparent plan to 'expose P as a target whereby we attack the B of A etc'.

The Concord police failed to publicise this find for the simple reason that it made little sense to them. And, because they didn't understand it, they did nothing to alert the Hearsts. The document wasn't handed over to the FBI for another month – by which time the action originally intended for 7 January and then deferred had been successfully carried out.

Not only did the police fail to make effective use of their finds, they also left valuable clues behind in the SLA hideout – and didn't think to place a guard there. The result was that a succession of 'visitors' looted the half-burned out house of much of its contents. Local children took whatever they could get their hands on, and they were followed by reporters. Marilyn Baker of San Francisco's KQED TV station was the first, and two of her finds led her to conclusions which would create potent myths about the SLA. First, her discovery of a case of theatrical make-up suggested to her that the SLA consisted of whites who passed themselves off as blacks. Second, her discovery that the words 'men and women' in an SLA leaflet had been altered to 'women and men' became the basis for a theory that the SLA was essentially a women's organisation with men relegated to a secondary role and black men in particular assigned the part of 'token blacks'. That militant feminism was a fundamental ingredient of the symbiosis is evident, but the merely fashionable transposition of 'men' and 'women' isn't in itself sufficient ground for the fanciful theory that Donald DeFreeze was in effect Mizmoon's manservant and the SLA's communal stud.

Another reporter who rummaged through the ashes at Sutherland Court was Carol Pogash of Randolph Hearst's paper, the *San Francisco Examiner*. She discovered enough to identify 'Nancy DeVoto' as Nancy Ling, and named her publicly on 13 January as 'the woman wanted in connection with the murder of Dr Marcus Foster'. Too late, the Concord police began to understand the importance of the case and posted guards on the house – but the looting went on. On 15 January two men drove up to the house and identified themselves as investigators from the office of Remiro's defence lawyer. The police guards let them in and watched as they loaded their van with all the remaining SLA papers and books. The two men turned out to be members of Venceremos and friends of some of the SLA activists.

But although they had allowed valuable clues to slip through their fingers, the police and FBI did at last have something on the mysterious and elusive terrorists of the Symbionese Liberation Army. They had two suspects behind bars, and they had the identity of the girl who, though they didn't know it, was the heart and perhaps the brain of the organisation. A week after the arrest of Little and Remiro they rumbled Little's substitution of Seventh Street for Seventh Avenue and raided the SLA's second hide-out. Although it was empty, there was evidence of SLA occupation. Then Little's former home, 'Peking House', was raided, yielding an M1 rifle, several hundred rounds of ammunition and the name of Little's co-resident, Willie Wolfe, who had suspiciously gone missing. The SLA was on the run.

From her new hiding place, which was probably Camilla Hall's as yet unmarked flat on Francisco Street, Nancy decided there was nothing to be lost in telling the world about the SLA.

On 19 January the *Examiner* received a 'Letter to the People' from 'Fahizah, former name Nancy Ling Perry'. Its five rambling, closely typed pages were turgid and lacked style, but despite its lack of literary merit the letter was to assume a special importance as the most personal statement of commitment to the SLA ever put on paper by one of its members.

Nancy began:

Greetings, my comrade sisters and brothers, all love, power and freedom to you. I am very glad to have this opportunity to speak to you, even though I know that what I am feeling cannot be completely expressed in words. You may have heard of me, not because I am any more important than any of you, but simply because my former name has been in the news lately. My name was Nancy Ling Perry, but my true name is Fahizah. What that name means is one who is victorious and I am one who believes in the liberation and victory of the people, because I have learned that what one really believes in is what will come to pass.

I am a freedom fighter in an information/intelligence unit of the United Federated Forces of the Symbionese Liberation Army. I still am that, in spite of the fact that I am now being sought for a political action, and in spite of the fact that two of my closest companeros are now chained in the Adjustment Center (the prison's prison) at San Quentin Concentration Camp. I am still with other members of the SLA information/intelligence unit, and I am hiding only from the enemy and not from the people. I have no intention of deserting my commitment nor would I ever try to run away from it, because I have learned that there is no flight to freedom except that of an armed projectile.

She went on to describe what she called 'the evolution of my consciousness', and in doing so laid bare the paranoid fantasies of the SLA's own peculiar brand of fringe-Left politics.

Basically, I have three backgrounds: I have a work background, a love background, and a prison background. My prison background means that I have close ties and feelings with our incarcerated brothers and sisters. What they have taught me is that if people on the outside do not understand the necessity of defending them through force of arms, then it is because these people on the outside do not yet realize that they are in an immediate danger of being thrown into concentration camps themselves, tortured or shot down in the

streets for expressing their beliefs. What my love background
has taught me was a whole lot of what love is all about, and
that the greater one's capacity for love is, the greater is one's
longing for freedom. What my work background taught me
is that one of the things that every revolutionary does is to
fight to get back the fruits of her or his own labor and the
control of his or her own destiny.

When I was in high school in 1963–64 I witnessed the first
military coup against we the people of this country. I saw us
passively sit by our TVs and unconsciously watch as the
militarily armed corporate state took over the existing government and blatantly destroyed the constitution that some of
us still believed in. I listened to the people around me deny
that a military coup had taken place and claim that such a
thing could not happen here. The people that I grew up
around were so politically naïve that their conceptions of a
military coup only recognized those that have occurred in
South America and African countries where the military and
ruling class took over the government by an open force of
arms. But the method of taking over the government was
different here. Here the coup was simply accomplished by
assassinating the then President John Kennedy, and then
assassinating any further opposition to the dictator who was
to take power: that dictator is the current President Richard
Nixon.

In 1964 I witnessed these and other somewhat hidden be-
ginnings of the military/corporate state which we now live
in. And I heard my teachers and the government-controlled
media spread lies about what had happened. I saw the Civil
Rights' Protests, the killings and bombings of my black
brothers and sisters and the conditioned reactions of extreme
racism in my school and home. When I questioned my
teachers about how these occurrences related to the meetings
of democracy and freedom that we were told existed to
protect us all, the answer I got was that we were better off not
knowing the truth about what was happening. I told my
teachers and my family and friends that I felt that we were
all being used as pawns and puppets, and that those who had

taken over the government were trying to keep us asleep and in a political stupor. I asked my teachers to tell me what happened in Nazi Germany; I asked them to tell me the meaning of fascism; I asked them to tell me the meaning of genocide; and when I began to hear about a war in Vietnam I asked them to tell me the meaning of imperialism. The answer to all my questions then was either silence or a reply filled with confusion and lies, and a racist pride and attitude that well, after all, it was all for us.

The experience of living in Amerikka has since taught me the realities of what fascism, imperialism and genocide meant; I have discovered the truth about the police state dictatorship, not because I studied about it in college, but because I see it every day, and because truth is something that is honestly known, as easily as beauty is seen. There is need for me to relate here everything that I have seen, or everything that I am sure you are already aware of. I am sure, my sisters and brothers, that you realize that the government is now in the rapid and steady process of removing the means of survival from the lower class and giving these benefits to the middle class in an effort to rally support from them. And as the government is removing these means of survival from the people, then naturally the people who have been robbed must in turn take back what rightfully belongs to them, and take back what they need in order to survive. This the current dictatorship calls a crime whether they take food from the grocery store, or take to the streets to make a speech, or take a gun in their hand to defend themselves.

This brought her to the subject of the Foster killing.

As a member of the Symbionese Liberation Army information intelligence unit, I fight against our common oppressor, and this I do with my gun as well as my mind. I try to use my mind and my imagination to uncover facts, so that when the SLA attacks it will be in the right place and that the actions of the more experienced SLA combat units will truly serve to benefit the people and answer their needs. The action taken by the SLA combat unit in reference to the Oakland Board of Education was a specific response to political police state programs and the failure of the Board to heed the rights and demands of the people in the community. The specific program was one of photo-identification (similar to the system of apartheid in South Africa), biological classification in the form of bio-dossiers which classify students according to race and political beliefs, internal warfare computerfiles, and armed police state patrols within the schools.

Intensely thorough intelligence operations carried out by one of the SLA information units was able to obtain factual information that Foster's signature was the first to appear on the Nixon Administration inspired proposals for armed police agents within certain Oakland schools and various forms of computer classification of students. Further intelligence revealed that Foster's background included membership on the Philadelphia Crime Commission. Foster's sideman Blackburn, is a CIA agent. As Director of Education in East Africa he worked to implement test programs against black people there, and he trained other agents to carry them out so that he could return to this country and introduce the same programs here.

I want to make it clear that the SLA was not indiscriminately issuing death warrents for Foster, Blackburn or anyone else, but rather we were attacking the programs and proposal of which they were the initiators, supporters and first signers. Such an attack was the only means left open to us to demand that the people's wishes be met, and that all such dangerous genocidal programs be stopped.

The government-controlled media has made some reference to the effect that this action was carried out by white people made up in black faces. Members of the SLA do not have to make up in black faces in order to defend the black community, since the SLA is a federation formed in the style of a revolutionary united nations whose commanding leadership is composed of representatives of the black, brown, yellow, red and white communities. We have more than enough members from every race to carry out any operation. As revolutionaries we would never disguise ourselves by race, because we would never deliberately act in a manner that would bring further police investigation onto any one race of peoples. But I would like to ask, since when does one have to be black in order to care about the murder of 14 year old Tyrone Guyton by political police state death squads, since when does one have to be white in order to feel for the starving children in Appalachia, since when does one have to be Asian in order to care about stopping the napalming of children in Vietnam, since when does one have to be brown in order to fight against the mass slaughters being conducted by the military junta in Chile???? Since when???? Not since we have come to realize that we are all one in struggle.

I am a member of the Symbionese Liberation Army information/intelligence unit, and that means that my responsibility is to aid the combat units with information, and keep myself armed at all times. I am in a race to learn how to fight, because I am in a race to survive. SLA people are confronted with oppression, starvation and the death of their freedom that they want to fight. It has been the history of many political leaders to suppress this will of the people, and to pretend that the people do not have the right to fight, and to pretend that the people will somehow achieve their liberation without revolutionary violence. But the truth is that there has never been a precedent for a non-violent revolution; the defenseless and unarmed people of Chile can testify to that.

All members of the SLA recognize that we right here in Amerikka are in a state of war, and that in a state of war, all must be armed and understand the true meaning of self-defense. When any member of the people's army strikes out at the murderer of our people and children, we are doing so in self-defense, we are doing so because we are left no alternative, and force of arms is now our only legal means to affect revolutionary justice. However, the natural instincts of many people in our country have become perverted by the conditionings to which they have been subjected, they have been conditioned to be afraid of revolutionary violence. I no longer have these fears because as a comrade of mine named

Osceola [Little] has taught me, 'The only way to destroy fear is to destroy the makers of fear, the murderer and the oppressor.' A revolutionary is not a criminal, nor is she or he an adventurer, and revolutionary violence is nothing but the most profound means of achieving internal as well as external balance . . .

All members of the SLA understand that politics are inseparable from struggle, in fact politics have no meaning without armed combat and information units to give politics a purpose. The Symbionese Liberation Army is unlike many existing political organizations in this country which support the armed liberation struggles of peoples throughout the world, but when it comes to the struggle here in Amerikka, they consistently denounce militancy and revolutionary violence and in so doing denounce the only means left to the people to achieve their liberation.

After this justification of revolutionary violence, Nancy offered her version of what had happened at Sutherland Court.

The house in Concord, California was a Symbionese Liberation Army information/intelligence headquarters, nothing more. The house was set on fire by me only to melt away any fingerprints that may have been overlooked. It never was intended that the fire would totally destroy the premises, because there was nothing left there that was of any real consequence to us, nor was there any material left behind that could stagnate the functioning ability of the SLA to carry on the struggle. The reports that mass armaments were found in that house is a lie. It is an attempt to frame my two comrade brothers and it is an assertion to cover up the fact that there were no weapons found there. All that remained were three broken BB guns [i.e. replicas], a couple of malfunctioning gas masks, a few research books, and several liberation posters on the walls.

Also, let me tell you that no-one living or coming to that house was a part of the SLA combat forces. This can be easily verified; first of all, everyone in SLA combat forces is offensively armed with cyanide bullets in all weapons that they carry; and up until today this had NOT been the case for SLA information/intelligence units or any support units. At that time all units but combat were only defensively armed with hand guns and carried no cyanide bullets. Secondly, we can easily verify that the ballistics on the .380 now in the hands of pig agents do not match those of the weapon used in the attack on the Oakland Board of Education. Information/intelligence units or any support units were never allowed to possess or have any contact with combat unit weapons. Beginning January 11th however, a directive was issued by the SLA and The Court of the People stating that as of that date, all units of the Symbionese Liberation Army are to be heavily, and offensively armed with cyanide bullets in all their weapons.

The letter ended with a message of encouragement to her lover, Little, and his companion, Remiro, in jail.

There really are no words available to me to express what I feel about the capture of my two companeros. They are in a concentration camp now because none of us were offensively armed, and because I was not aware that they were under attack. But my beautiful brothers, as we have said many times, we learn from our mistakes, and we learn from our active participation in struggle, not from political rhetoric, so we won't cry, but simply fight on; and right on with that. A comrade of mine, Bo, says something that I'd like to leave you with: 'There are two things to remember about revolution. We are going to get our asses kicked – and we are going to win.'

Death to the Fascist insect that preys upon the life of the people – Fahizah.

The *Examiner* ran only a short summary, which was all the letter seemed worth to the duty sub. He could hardly have foreseen that, three weeks later, the paper would be compelled to print the letter again, taking special care not to omit a single comma.

4 Kidnapped

It happened that on the very day the SLA sent out their 'Declaration of Revolutionary War', 21 August 1973, Congressman Richard H. Ichord, chairman of the House Committee on Internal Security, noted in the committee's report that the United States had been fortunate to escape the rash of political kidnappings which had occurred in Latin America and elsewhere since 1968. But he went on to warn against the complacent attitude that 'it cannot happen here'.

The kidnap weapon was a frequent topic of conversation among far-Left groups and armchair revolutionaries. The notion of using hostages to force, say, the release of prisoners had a beguiling simplicity for those who had lost faith in the more complex politics of persuasion. If the hostage came to any harm it was because he had been callously abandoned by his friends. His blood would be on their hands, not those of his captors.

So kidnapping became a common fantasy among the radical underground, finding its way, along with the theft of an H-bomb or subversion of the White House, into any number of crazed scenarios for instant revolution. It was also popular in underground fiction. A hard-core porn novel called *Black Abductor*, published in 1972, told the story of 'Patricia', daughter of a wealthy Californian family, who is kidnapped, communicates with her parents via communiqués published in the media, is seduced by her captors and joins forces with them. The book was soon to be of special interest to the FBI – and not only to its vice squad.

Kidnapping was one of the subjects introduced into Vaca-ville's BCA sessions in the spring and early summer of 1973. Among potential victims discussed by the prisoners were the daughters of the California prison chief Raymond Procunier and of the then Vice-President Gerald Ford. Daughters were popular with both male and female revolutionaries: with men, perhaps, because they could be fantasised as sexual as well as political victims, and with women for the more practical reason that girls were likely to be more controllable than men.

None of the early SLA documents had shown a strong commitment to the strategy of political kidnapping. It was only after the Foster killing had proved disastrous in propaganda terms that the group turned to a tactic popularised by the Tupamaros and their imitators. The papers found in the Con-cord hide-out suggest that businessmen and prison officers were the first targets considered by the SLA. Then they seem to have turned over a handful of prominent daughters. By Christmas, Patty Hearst was in their focus.

Why Patty? It has been suggested that the announcement of her engagement to Steven Weed put her briefly in the public eye, and so in the eye of the SLA. It is possible that the SLA picked up a gossip paragraph in one of San Francisco's underground papers highlighting Patty's remarks to her father that no one under eighty read his papers. Another theory, pursued but soon abandoned by the FBI, was that Emily Harris, through her work as a temporary typist at the University, had access to Patty's confidential file in which it is suggested there may have been information which could have led the SLA to believe that she might become a willing convert. However, the university denied that a junior typist in Emily's position could gain access to the files, and in any case it is unlikely that the thought of making a convert of their hostage ever entered the SLA's calculations before the kidnapping.

The most likely explanation is the simplest one: that the SLA, having decided to kidnap the daughter of a family wealthy enough to pay up a large ransom, settled on Patty Hearst because her father was both sufficiently wealthy and a newspaper tycoon. To kidnap Patty Hearst was also to kidnap the media. And there she was, living unprotected in the middle of the Berkeley community, conveniently up for grabs.

On 15 January, five days after the arrest of Little and Remiro, Bill Harris wrote from his hiding place a letter to a black prisoner in San Quentin. He signed it 'Dorothy'. 'Conditions are certainly not good for us getting together. I want you to know I am fine and stronger than ever, despite some recent setbacks. We intend to overcome the setbacks in a powerful manner.'

On the evening of Sunday, 3 February, a young couple knocked on the door of Steven Weed's apartment. Patty was out. Steven answered the door and the couple enquired whether there were any vacant flats in the building. Having cased the apartment, Emily Harris and her unidentified companion drove off to report back to their comrades.

The following evening, a thirty-one-year-old laboratory mathematician named Peter Benenson was in his garage tinkering with his old Chevrolet Impala. The garage led on to a courtyard surrounded by a brick wall which, on its further side, enclosed the patio of the Weed-Hearst apartment.

Just after nine o'clock, Benenson became aware of two black men standing at the entrance to the garage. They were armed. One of them demanded the car keys; the other told Benenson to turn to the wall with his hands behind his back. Wondering why anyone should choose to steal his battered old car, Benenson nevertheless did what he was told. His hands and feet were tied and he was bundled into the back of the car, where he was blindfolded. The car reversed into the courtyard. In the apartment on the other side of the wall, Patty was taking a shower in preparation for an early night.

At 9.20, Steven heard a tap at the window. A girl was calling that there had been an accident and could she please use the telephone. Weed opened the door and two black men armed with rifles burst into the apartment, followed by the girl at the window. According to Weed's account, 'In seconds they had me face down on the floor in the hallway. They kept kicking me in the face and forcing me to keep my head down.' One snatched his wallet, containing a little money and his passport. The other ran upstairs and Weed heard Patty screaming before he began to lose consciousness.

A neighbour, Steven Suenaga, heard the commotion and ran into the apartment. He too was beaten up and knocked to the ground. Another neighbour, hearing the noise, looked out of his window to see two men carrying a girl out of the house. 'She was struggling. She was half-dressed, naked from the waist up. She screamed, "Please let me go." I think she was blindfolded.'

Other frightened neighbours were at their windows or doorways in time to see Patty dropped into the boot of Peter Benenson's Chevrolet. As the car lurched off, a fusilade of shots was fired from an M1 rifle towards the apartment building.

Six blocks away the Chevrolet was abandoned and Patty was transferred to an estate wagon, driven by Mizmoon. Benenson was left, still tied and blindfolded, on the back seat of his car. Somehow, he told the police later, he managed to work himself free. When the car was found it was empty. He didn't call the police to tell them what had happened till next morning, explaining that he was 'too terrified'. Suspicious, the police reported that he had 'exhibited a hostile attitude' and they had been 'unable to secure his full, willing co-operation'. It was several weeks before they grudgingly dropped the idea that he was a willing accomplice. From eye-witness descriptions the police were able to put together composite sketches of their suspects. Later they put names to their inadequate identikit pictures: Angela Atwood, Donald DeFreeze and Thero Wheeler.

On the day after the kidnapping, with Patty missing and Weed in hospital, the FBI turned over the apartment. In the bedroom they found some pot, but in the living-room they made a more curious discovery. Tucked neatly under the stereo set was a small carton of cyanide-tipped bullets. The SLA had left a visiting card.

*

Randolph Hearst was called at Hillsborough just before ten o'clock. He immediately made his way first to Patty's apartment and then, with a police escort, to the hospital where Weed had been taken. There he had a telephone conference with senior Berkeley police chiefs which resulted in an agreement that there would be no publicity till the unknown kidnappers had shown their hand.

Hearst was in a position to ensure that his own *Examiner* would keep quiet, but he could do no more than request the co-operation of papers outside his chain. Gordon Pates, Managing Editor of the *Chronicle*, which shared editorial and printing facilities with the *Examiner*, agreed immediately, but Senator William Knowland, who ran the rival *Oakland Tribune* across the Bay, was harder to persuade and agreed only after a combined appeal from Hearst and the police.

So the early editions of the *Chronicle* and *Tribune*, followed by the first mid-morning edition of the *Examiner*, carried nothing on the dramatic events of the previous evening (though the *Chronicle* did run a letter purporting to come from the SLA and threatening more mass killings, the first of many hoax communiqués). But over breakfast, Senator Knowland had second thoughts. He rang Berkeley police press executive Richard Berger to tell him that since there had been a score of witnesses to the incident, and since the whole neighbourhood had heard the shots, and since half the Berkeley campus had some version of the story, he was going to run it in his evening edition. More personal appeals from members of the Hearst family failed to dissuade him. Reluctantly, Hearst and the police decided they had no alternative but to lift the attempted embargo, and at 10.30 am the local KGO radio news broke the story: William Randolph Hearst's granddaughter had been carried off naked by armed blacks.

The story shot a spasm of terror into wealthy families across America. In their high-security apartment blocks, patrolled by private armies of guards, the rich and the famous realised how vulnerable their student children were, living in the unprotected and unprotectable world of a university campus. Some sons and daughters were called home, others urged to keep guns in their rooms. Men who had never been modest about their wealth and status asked newspaper editors to stop describing them as wealthy. Tycoons became mere businessmen, and across the nation mansions were demoted to houses.

Two days after the kidnap, Randolph and Catherine Hearst appeared on television to make an emotional plea to the unknown kidnappers to return Patty unharmed. Mrs Hearst was wearing black. Steven Weed announced from hospital that he would not testify against the kidnappers if Patty were freed.

They got their answer next day. It came in the form of another communiqué, one copy of which was addressed to Berkeley radio station KPFA and the other to a student paper, the *Berkeley Barb*. The radio station's copy was accompanied by one of Patty's credit cards, taken from her handbag which had been snatched from the apartment.

Again purporting to come from the 'Western Regional Adult Unit' of the SLA, the communiqué took the form of a 'Warrant Order issued by The Court of the People' for the 'arrest and protective custody, and if resistance, execution', of 'Patricia Campbell Hearst, daughter of Randolph Hearst, corporate enemy of the people'. It was dated 4 February, the day of the kidnapping, and announced:

On the afore-stated date, combat elements of the United Federated Forces of the Symbionese Liberation Army armed with cyanide-loaded weapons served an arrest warrant upon Patricia Campbell Hearst. It is the order of this court that the subject be arrested by combat units and removed to a protective area of safety . . .

It is the directive of this court that during this action only, no civilian elements be harmed if possible, and that warning shots be given. However, if any citizens attempt to aid the authorities or interfere with the implementation of this order, they shall be executed immediately. This court hereby notifies the public and directs all combat units in the future to shoot to kill any civilian who attempts to witness or interfere with any operation conducted by the people's forces against the fascist state.

Then came the specific threat against Patty:

Should any attempt be made by authorities to rescue the prisoner, or to arrest or harm any SLA elements, the prisoner is to be executed.

The prisoner is to be maintained in adequate physical and mental condition, and unharmed as long as these conditions are adhered to. Protective custody shall be composed of combat and medical units, to safeguard both the prisoner and her health.

Then came the paragraph which was to hold the press, radio and television hardly less captive than Patty:

All communiqués from this court *MUST* be published in full, in all newspapers, and all other forms of the media. Failure to do so will endanger the safety of the prisoner. Further communications will follow.

The communiqué was simply signed 'SLA' and ended with the slogan, 'Death to the fascist insect that preys upon the life of the people'.

If the Hearsts and the public now knew that Patty's kidnappers were the SLA, that didn't leave them much wiser. Who and what was the SLA? Newspaper readers in the Bay area who had followed the Foster case knew that two of its members had been charged with that killing and that a girl named Nancy Ling Perry was being sought by the police. Outside California, across America and the rest of the world, the SLA had scarcely been heard of. Two thousand miles away in Washington, US Attorney-General William Saxbe, promising a massive FBI enquiry, conceded that law enforcement officials knew nothing about the group. 'They talk about a liberating force,' he grumbled, 'but nobody knows what they want to liberate.' He speculated that they were probably tied up with the black secret society which was currently terrorising the Bay Area with random race killings, code named by the police, 'Zebra'.

The press speculated too, but with more caution, terrified of running stories which might unwittingly endanger Patty's life. The *Chronicle*'s Tim Findley had already written a story tentatively identifying Donald DeFreeze as an SLA member, and the *Examiner*'s Carol Pogash, who had been the first to name Nancy Ling Perry, now had leads on other women members. But both stories were spiked as potentially provocative. Findley was soon to quit in protest against his editor's caution, but Pogash was more philosophical: 'You can't expect a father to choose his business over his daughter.'

On 9 February the SLA's demand that its own version of events be 'published in full' was put to its first test. A reporter on the *Palo Alto Times* received a telephone call from a woman who said she belonged to the SLA and was known by the code name 'Sanzinga'. The woman was never identified but may have been Nancy herself, the reporter perhaps mishearing 'Fahizah'. The *Examiner*, she said, had made a serious mistake in not publishing in full Nancy's 'Letter to the People' of 11 January. Next morning it ran the full text.

The same day, Russell Little's father offered to trade himself for Patty. A number of Left superstars with an eye for publicity were emboldened to offer a similar self-sacrifice in the coming weeks. The SLA ignored them.

A week after the kidnap there was still no indication of what conditions the SLA would set for Patty's release. It was widely assumed that they would offer a straight swap for Little and Remiro, and Randolph Hearst had anticipated this by taking legal advice on what might legitimately be done for the two SLA men in San Quentin. This led to exploratory talks with California's ultra-conservative Governor Ronald Reagan, a family friend and the only man constitutionally empowered to set Little and Remiro free without a court order. Reagan told Hearst that his police advisers were adamantly opposed to such an exchange.

Hearst was preparing to organise a lobby to persuade the Governor to change his mind when the SLA stepped in with their fourth communiqué. It arrived in the mail at radio station KPFA on 12 February. The SLA's demands proved infinitely more ambitious than Hearst or Reagan could ever have expected but, sensational as they were, it was what came with the communiqué that attracted most attention.

It was a cassette tape recording, and it carried the unmistakable voice of Patty Hearst, subdued and tired, but controlled and unhysterical. She talked for nearly fifteen minutes with several apparent tape stops, evidently speaking off the cuff rather than reading a prepared statement.

She began by assuring her parents she was alive and as well as could be expected:

Mom, Dad, I am OK. I had a few scrapes and stuff, but they washed them up and they are getting OK. I have caught a cold but they are giving me some pills for it. So I'm not being starved or beaten or unnecessarily frightened. I've heard some press reports and know that Steve and all the neighbours are OK and that no one was really hurt.

But the SLA, said Patty, was 'very upset about press distortions'. It had not been 'shooting innocent people in the streets'. She went on, speaking more hesitantly:

I am kept blindfolded so I can't identify anyone, and my hands are often tied, but not – not generally, they're not. And . . . um . . . I am not gagged or anything. I am comfortable. I think you can tell that I am not really terrified or anything. And I am OK.

Then came the first indication of what *did* frighten her. A few days earlier Oakland police had burst into an empty apartment suspected of being an SLA hideout. No doubt her captors had given her a highly coloured account of the incident, or she may have seen the dramatic television news pictures of the police, shooting their way in. Clearly it worried her.

I was very upset . . . to hear about the police rushing in on that house in Oakland and I was just really glad that I wasn't there. I would appreciate it if everyone would just calm down and not try to find me and not be making identifications

because they are not only endangering me but they are endangering themselves. I am with a combat unit that's armed
with automatic weapons and there is also a medical team
here and there is no way that I will be released until they let
me go. So it wouldn't do any good for somebody to come in
here and try to get me by force.

These people aren't just a bunch of nuts. They have been
really honest with me, but they are perfectly willing to die
for what they are doing. I want to get out of here, but the
only way I am going to is if we do it their way. And I just
hope that you'll do what they say, Dad, and do it quickly.

The tape clicked a couple of times, 'I have been stopping
and starting this tape myself,' explained Patty conversationally,
'so I can collect my thoughts. That's why there are so many
stops in it.' Then, guessing what would now be in her parents'
minds, she went on:

I am not being forced to say any of this and I think it is
really important that you take their requests very seriously
about not arresting any SLA members and about following
their good faith request to the letter. And I just want to get
out of here and see everyone again and be back with Steve.

The SLA is very interested in seeing how you are taking
this, Dad, and they want to make sure you are really serious
and listening to what they are saying and they think that you
have been taking this whole thing a lot more seriously than
the police and FBI and other federal people have been taking
it.

It seems to be getting to the point where they're not
worried about you so much as they are worrying about other
people, or at least I am.

It is – it is really up to you to make sure that these people
don't jeopardise my life by charging in and doing stupid
things, and I hope that you will make sure that they don't do
anything else like that Oakland house business.

Pretty soon – the SLA people have been honest with me
and I feel pretty sure that I am going to get out of here if

everything goes the way they want it to. And I think you
should feel that way too. And try not to worry so much. I
mean, I know it is hard, but I heard that Mom was really
upset and everybody was at home. And I hope that this puts
you a little bit at ease and that you know that I really am all
right. I just hope I can get back to everybody really soon.

Then in a curious passage that was to be the focus of much
speculation, Patty gave a straightforward account of her captors'
ideological standpoint. The SLA, she said, had 'ideological ties
with the IRA' and other movements 'struggling for independence'. They 'considered themselves soldiers' she said, which
made her a prisoner of war, 'like the two men in San Quentin'.

I am here because I am a member of a ruling-class family
and I think you can begin to see the analogy. The people, the
two men in San Quentin, are being held and they are going to
be tried simply because they are members of the SLA and
not because they have done anything. Witnesses to the shooting of Foster saw black men, and two white men have been
arrested for this, and you're being told this so that you will
understand why I was kidnapped. And so that you will
understand that whatever happens to the two prisoners is
going to happen to me. You have to understand that I am
held to be innocent in the same way those two men in San
Quentin are innocent. That they are simply members of a
group and have not actually done anything themselves to
warrant their arrest. They apparently are part of an intelligence unit and have never executed anyone themselves.
The SLA has declared war against the government and it's
important that you understand that they know what they are
doing and they understand what their actions mean and that
you realise that this is not considered by them to be a simple
kidnapping and that you don't treat it that way and say you
don't know why I was kidnapped.
I am telling you why this happened so that you will know
and so that you will have something to use, some knowledge
to get me out of here. If you can get the food thing organised

before the 19th, then that's OK and that would just speed up my release.

Today is Friday the 8th and in Kuwait the commandos have negotiated the release of their hostages and left the country. Bye.

Patty's casual reference to 'the food thing' was explained by the first of two male voices on the same tape. The speaker identified himself as 'General Field-Marshal Cinque, known to my comrades as Cin,' and after a bitter attack on 'the fascist media empire of the ultra-Right Hearst Corporation' and on Mrs Hearst's role on the University of California Board of Regents, he went on to put the SLA's unique and sensational demand.

The SLA have arrested the subject for the crimes that her mother and father have, by their action, committed against we, the American people and the oppressed people of the world . . .

It is therefore the directive of this court that before any form of negotiations for the release of the subject prisoner be initiated, that an action of good faith be shown on the part of the Hearst family, and in so doing show some form of repentance for the murder and suffering they have aided and profited from . . .

This gesture is to be in the form of food to the needy and the unemployed.

Cinque left no doubt as to what would follow if the 'gesture' were not forthcoming:

We are not savage killers and madmen and we do hold a high moral value to life . . . But speaking as a father, I am quite willing to lose both my children if by that action I could save thousands of white, black, yellow, and red children from a life of suffering, exploitation and murder. And I am therefore quite willing to carry out the execution of your daughter to save the life of starving men, women and children of every race . . .

And if, as you and others so naïvely believe, that we will lose, let it be known that even in death we will win, for the very ashes of this fascist nation will mark our graves.

The second male voice, heavily distorted but believed to be Bill Harris, ended the tape with a warning that

Uh, Mr Hearst . . . the police authorities and others are attempting to place the responsibility upon us concerning the life of your daughter . . . However, whatever happens to your daughter will be totally your responsibility and the responsibility of the authorities which you represent. Her life will be maintained in the fashion that is accorded to the terms of war, and if they and yourself violate these, her life and blood will be upon your hands only.

The communiqué accompanying the tape demanded that not only the letter itself but also the transcripts of the tape, the text of the cobra leaflet and the 'Declaration of Revolutionary War' be published in full by 'all newspapers and other forms of the media'. First to comply was the *Chronicle*. 'Suppose you don't and the girl gets killed,' commented Managing Editor Gordon Pates, 'what do you do, argue freedom of the press?' The *Examiner* followed, giving over 440 column inches to the SLA, spread over three pages. Hearst himself vetoed a suggestion that the documents be printed in small type, and had the type-written communiqué published in facsimile. He also added a note of his own saying that the 'co-operation' of other Hearst papers and broadcasting stations had been sought and obtained, and that the owners of the 1700 newspapers *not* controlled by the Hearst Corporation had been sent an appeal to 'co-operate to the greatest extent possible'. Very few papers, most of them small and remote, declined to do so. Pates's explanation on behalf of the *Chronicle* became for the next few weeks the guide and rationale for almost the entire American press.

The result was that the tiny band making up the SLA received more unedited, uncritical coverage of its half-baked programme than the whole of the traditional Left had received for orthodox socialism in a decade, perhaps in a century. While this no doubt delighted the SLA and amused the underground papers, it also provoked an angry backlash from the Right. In Washington, Attorney-General Saxbe, angered as much by Patty's uncomplimentary and ungrateful references to the police as by the media's capitulation to terrorist blackmail, bluntly told newsmen that if Federal investigators found out where Patty was being held it would be a dereliction of duty not to 'go get her'. For good measure, he advised Hearst not to give in to the group's vague and unrealistic demands for a food programme for the needy. Hearst responded angrily: 'To make a statement from faraway Washington that you are going to bust in and shoot the place up is damned near irresponsible.'

Patty had expressed two fears. One was of just the kind of police 'bust-in' which Saxbe promised and the other was of SLA reaction if they were identified by name in the press. Until the tape, newsmen had reluctantly withheld the identifications they had been able to make as a result of their own investigations. Findley of the *Chronicle* had seen a story on DeFreeze spiked and Marilyn Baker of KQED TV, having turned up the names of DeFreeze and Wheeler, had agreed after a personal intervention by Hearst not to name them in her news report.

But the arrival of the tape changed all that. At the *Chronicle* it was argued that Cinque had in effect identified himself, since scores of people in Berkeley and Vacaville knew 'Cinque' to be the assumed name of one Donald DeFreeze. Once this was put to Hearst, he reluctantly dropped his objection and called KQED to tell them so. On the evening of 14 February, Marilyn Baker went on the air to name the SLA leader as Donald DeFreeze, escaped convict. Tim Findley's story for the *Chronicle* the following morning went further. Recalling the comments of some Berkeley community groups that DeFreeze 'came on so heavy that he might be a provocateur', Findley began to open up the conspiracy-theory aspects of the story – only to have this section cut out by a nervous sub. Nevertheless, within ten days of Patty's kidnapping, the mysterious SLA, thought protected by its captive editors, had begun, with the naming of its 'field-marshal', to assume a human face.

Down in Los Angeles, 400 miles south, the name Donald DeFreeze must have jogged some memories in the Los Angeles Police Department, not least with Detective Robert Farwell's 'Black Desk' in the Criminal Conspiracy Section. And it might, too, have rung alarm bells in the office of State Attorney-General Evelle J. Younger, who as Los Angeles County District Attorney had created the CCS and had later found himself on the end of an attempted subpoena when DeFreeze was tried in 1970. But if Younger did recall that the SLA's 'General Field-Marshal' had, four years earlier, been one of his own police department's spies, he kept quiet about it. Certainly when Younger called Randolph Hearst to reassure him that everything possible was being done to find and protect his daughter, he did not reveal that the man who held her was, at least in part, a product of police counter-subversion training. And in public, Younger's only comments on the SLA affair were to the effect that the FBI seemed to have gone soft on kidnapping.

The notion of a free food programme for the needy, as demanded by DeFreeze, was not the invention of the SLA. Since the mid-sixties, first 'community politics' then 'street politics' had absorbed much of the idealism and energy of the New Left, the more so as global issues like Vietnam began to seem less and less amenable to individual influence and initiative.

From 1966 on, the poorer areas of San Francisco and Oakland had become used to invasions of assorted liberal groups, Yippies, Hippies and 'street people' vying with each other to run free food centres, free clothes stores, free clinics. After 1968 the Black Panthers themselves turned to a similar strategy in black areas, seeking both to expand their popular base and to create a revolutionary consciousness in their followers.

What was new about the SLA demand was its colossal scale and, of course, the means by which the programme was to be financed. What the SLA described as 'a symbolic gesture of good faith' was required to take the form of a free gift of $70 worth of 'top quality meats, vegetables and dairy products' to 'all people with welfare cards, social security pension cards, food stamp cards, disabled veteran cards, medical cards, parole or probation papers, and jail or bail release slips'.

To avoid long queues, said the SLA, distribution must take place every Tuesday, Thursday and Saturday for four weeks. Five distribution centres must be set up in each of the communities chosen by the SLA as beneficiaries of the scheme: the Mission, Chinatown, Hunters Point and Fillmore districts of San Francisco; East and West Oakland; Richmond, East Palo Alto, Delano, Santa Rosa; and the Watts, Compton and East districts of Los Angeles.

The SLA communiqué also specified the community groups it wanted as 'observers and co-ordinators' of the programme. They included the Black Panther Party and a dozen local black, women's, prisoners' and welfare organisations. Their job was 'to see to it that the aged and disabled receive their food and ways to transport it and shop for it, and to see to it that NO police-state agents, in or out of uniform, are allowed to be in the areas of food distribution or photograph or harass people.' Intended recipients were told: 'If you are not receiving your food, all you have to do is voice your discontent in the streets, at bus stops, movie theatres etc and we will hear about it.'

Randolph Hearst, immediately after receiving the tape, began drafting a statement saying he would be glad to comply. But the fact was that Hearst had little idea how many people were 'needy' according to the SLA's definitions. He thought in terms of thousands, which would have meant that the ransom was well within his reach. However some of his advisers had other ideas. State Attorney Younger and FBI local bureau chief Charles Bates were opposed to what they saw as a second abject surrender. The SLA had secured all the media coverage it demanded; must it now be given the full propaganda victory? Would not such a course encourage further demands, both from the SLA itself and from imitators?

If Hearst had underestimated the scale and cost, Younger and Bates overestimated it. Taking the whole State of California (though the SLA communiqué was concerned only with parts of the Bay Area and part of Los Angeles) they pointed out that

there were nearly six million people who could qualify by the
SLA's definition as 'needy'. To give nearly six million people
$70 worth of food each would cost $415 million. That
was enough to keep 155 supermarkets fully stocked for a year;
or enough to pay the whole of San Francisco's grocery bill for
four years.

The figures stunned Randolph Hearst. They far exceeded the
combined value of his personal assets and even those of the
Hearst Corporation. He was a millionaire, but not 415 times
over. On 13 February, the day after the SLA's demand was
received, he told newsmen that it was physically and financially
impossible to meet the kidnappers' demands. Younger, Bates
and the conservative hard-liners had pulled back a round.

Hearst also appealed to the SLA to release Patty, promising
he would then 'forget the whole thing'. But Younger stepped
in quickly to say that no one had the authority to forget a breach
of the law. Bates backed him with an assertion that the SLA
was a criminal gang and 'you can't compromise with hoods'.

The SLA had its reply ready. That same morning the Rev
Cecil Williams, a black pastor and radical activist, received an
anonymous telephone call telling him to go to a phone booth
in the garage of the Hilton Hotel, near the San Francisco
Downtown Air Terminal.

Williams' Glide Memorial Church was one of the community
groups designated by the SLA as 'observers and co-ordinators'
of the food programme. Three days before the SLA called him,
he had arranged a secret meeting with other community leaders
to put together a plan by which he would offer his services as
mediator between the Hearsts and the SLA. 'I don't know who
the SLA are,' he had told reporters, 'but I understand what
they are saying.'

Following the instructions of his anonymous caller, he found
in the phone booth an envelope containing the key to locker
531 at the air terminal. In the locker he found another cassette
tape from the SLA.

That afternoon, for the second time in four days, the Hearsts
listened to the recorded voice of their daughter.

Dad, Mom, I'm making this tape to let you know that I'm still OK and to explain a few things, I hope.

First about the good faith gesture. There was some misunderstanding about that and you should do what you can and they understand that you want to meet their demands and they have every intention that you should be able to meet their demands.

They weren't trying to present an unreasonable request. It was never intended that you feed the whole state. So whatever you come up with basically is OK. And just do it as fast as you can and everything will be fine ...

Also I would like to emphasise that I am alive and that I am well and that in spite of what certain tape experts seem to think, I mean I'm fine.

It's really depressing to hear people talk about me like I'm dead. I can't explain what that's like. What it does also, is that it . . . it begins to convince other people that maybe I am dead.

If everybody is convinced that I am dead, well that gives the FBI an excuse to come in here and try to pull me out. I'm sure that Mr Bates understands that if the FBI has to come in and get me out by force that they won't have time to decide who not to kill. They'll just have to kill everyone.

I don't particularly want to die that way.

So I hope you'll realise that everything is OK and just back off for a while. There's plenty of time for investigation later.

Then followed the passage that began, for the first time, to open up a new and mysterious dimension to what had hitherto been a more or less straightforward kidnap story. Patty, although previously uncritical of her kidnappers' ideological view, now sought to excuse and even justify their actions.

This is basically an example, a symbolic warning, not to you but to everyone, that there are people who are not going to accept your support of other governments and that faced with suppression and murder of the people . . . this is a warning to everybody.

It's also to show what can be done. That when it's necessary the people can be fed and to show that it's too bad it has to happen this way to make people see that there are people who need food.

Now maybe something can be done about that, so that things like this won't have to happen again.

Also, the SLA is very annoyed about attempts by the press and by authorities to turn this into a racial issue. It's not. This is a political issue and this is a political action that they've taken.

Anyone who really reads the stated objectives of the SLA can see very clearly that this is not a racial thing. I hope there won't be any more confusion about that.

I turned over my notes there so . . .

I am being held as a prisoner of war and not as anything else and I'm being treated in accordance with international codes of war. And so you shouldn't listen or believe what anybody else says about the way I'm being treated. This is the way I'm being treated. I'm not left alone and I'm not just shoved off. I mean, I am fine.

I am not being starved and I'm not being beaten or tortured. Really.

Since I am an example, it's really important that everybody understands that I am an example and a warning. And because of this, it's very important to the SLA that I return safely. So people should stop acting like I'm dead.

Mom should get out of her black dress. That doesn't help at all.

I wish you'd try to understand the position I'm in. I'm right in the middle and I have to depend upon what all kinds of other people are going to do.

And it's really hard for me to hear about reports, you know, and . . . I hope you understand and try to do something.

I know that a lot of people have written and everyone is concerned about me and my safety and about what you're going through, and I want them all to know that I'm OK.

And it's important for them to understand that I'll be OK

as long as the SLA demands are met, and as long as the two
prisoners at San Quentin are OK.

And as long as the FBI don't come in here. That is my
biggest worry. I think I can get out of here alive as long as
they don't come busting in and I really think you should
understand that the SLA does have an interest in my return.

And try not to worry so much and just do what you can. I
mean I know you're doing everything. Take care of Steve and
hurry. Bye.

The message closed with a dating device: 'On Wednesday,
Solzhenitsyn was exiled to West Germany.'

At the end of the tape were a few words from DeFreeze,
tossing the ball back into Hearst's court.

This is General Field-Marshal Cin speaking. We wish to
clarify what your daughter has said about our request for a
good faith gesture on your part. The people are awaiting
your gesture. You may rest assured that we are quite able to
assess the extent of your sincerity in this matter and we will
accept a sincere effort on your part.

We are quite able and aware of the extent of your capabilities as we are also aware of the needs of the people.

Death to the fascist insect that preys upon the life of the
people!

So now the screws were on. Instead of being cowed by the
hard line Younger and Bates had foisted on Hearst, the SLA
had left the next, crucial move to Hearst. He had to decide the
extent of the programme, manoeuvred suddenly into the curious
position where not only the SLA but Patty herself seemed to
challenge him to assess her worth. In another impromptu press
conference on the steps of his Hillsborough home, he told newsmen, 'I'll move as fast as I can and let them know what I can
do.'

Earlier in the week, taking his first steps towards finding an
experienced full-time organiser to run the food programme,
Hearst had approached Ludlow Kramer, Secretary of State for

Patty before the kidnapping
(United Press International Photo)

Far left: Donald David DeFreeze on the Hibernia bank raid - a gun under his donkey jacket
(United Press International Photo)

Left: Willie Wolfe; below: Angela Atwood
(United Press International Photo)

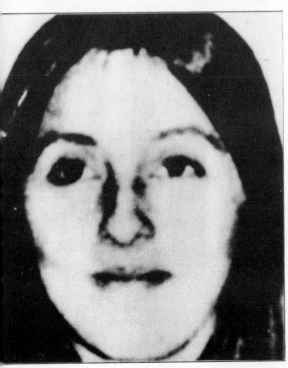

Above left: Nancy Ling Perry *(Popperfoto)*; above right: Camilla Hall *(United Press International Photo)*; below left: Patricia 'Mizmoon' Soltysik *(United Press International Photo)*; below right: Emily Harris *(Associated Press Photo)*

Opposite page: Joseph Remiro (in front) and Russell Little, both in handcuffs, being led from court after facing a murder charge *(United Press International Photo)*

Right: Donald De-
Freeze; below: Bill
Harris *(Associated
Press Photo)*

Far right: Catherine
and Randolph Hearst
- the parents who
still wait *(United
Press International
Photo)*

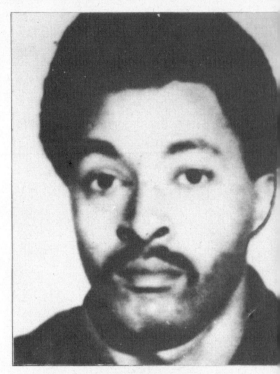

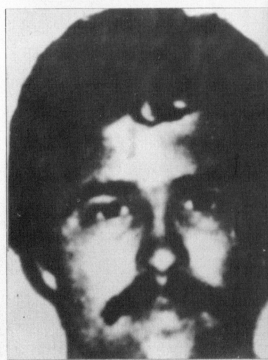

Far left: Patty during
the Hibernia raid
(Popperfoto)

Left: Steven Weed,
Patty's fiancé, five
days after being
beaten up during
Patty's kidnapping
with Catherine
Hearst *(Popperfoto)*

Below: Members of
the Los Angeles
Police 'SWAT' squad
covering the house
where DeFreeze and
five other members
of the SLA died
*(United Press Inter-
national Photo)*

Right: Free food being thrown to the crowd during the multimillion dollar distribution, ordered by the SLA *(United Press International Photo)*

Below: Pro SLA posters on a bulletin board on the Berkeley campus, April 1974 *(Popperfoto)*

WE LOVE

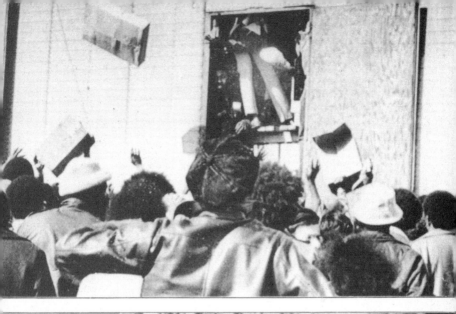

Time: Monday, Thursday 4:30 - 6:00
Place: Ballet Arts Center 4684 Telegraph
Phone: 653-0684   Introductory class
April 11, $1.00, thereafter $20. for 4 wks.
Instructor: William Tobias

7800

WE LOVE YOU

WE LOVE YO

TANIA

ANGELA Y. DAVIS

Slogans on the wall of the SLA's deserted San Francisco hideout
'Freedom is the will of life', signed Cinque; and 'Patria o Muerte. Venceremos',
signed Tania *(United Press International Photo)*

the State of Washington, who had recently run a successful 'Neighbours In Need' programme among his own State's un-employed. Kramer had said he would have to think about it: he was planning to run for Congress and wanted time to consider the political consequences of seeming to be, in the eyes of his conservative constituents, the executive arm of a band of revolutionary terrorists.

After the arrival of Patty's second tape, Hearst pressed Kramer for an immediate decision, and he agreed. On 19 February Hearst told a press conference that Kramer would head a 'People In Need' (PIN) programme to which $2 million would be allocated. Half a million dollars – 'a substantial part, maybe more than a quarter of my assets' – would come from his own pocket. The other million-and-a-half would come from the funds of the $74 million-strong William Randolph Hearst Foundation.

'The SLA has asked us to make a gesture of good will,' said Hearst, 'and I expect them to make a gesture of sincerity them-selves.' Next day, 20 February, was Patty's twentieth birthday. 'I'll be waiting for her in a nice bright dress,' said Mrs Hearst, who had hastily abandoned the black dress that Patty had com-plained of and was wearing a bright pink blouse under a blue coat.

That afternoon, Randolph Hearst had his first private meeting with leaders of the radical groups nominated by the SLA to observe and co-ordinate the programme. Among those present were the Rev Cecil Williams, Dennis Banks of the American Indian Movement and representatives of the Black Panthers. It was a unique occasion: a white millionaire and a multi-racial collection of revolutionaires earnestly discussing how best to redistribute two million dollars. The meeting, his first face-to-face encounter with radical America, moved Hearst deeply. The radicals in turn were impressed with Hearst's sincerity, and particularly with his acknowledgement that 'the real problems go much deeper than food and go into jobs and job placements, which we'll have to do something about when this is all over.'

But if Hearst impressed the topside radicals, he wasn't moving fast or far enough for the SLA. Patty wasn't released on her birthday. Instead, the SLA placed a new tape in the ladies' lavatory at the San Francisco Public Library where, until only a few weeks earlier, Mizmoon had been working as a temporary cleaner.

Patty's only words on this tape were the dating device: 'Today is the 19th and yesterday the Shah of Iran had two people executed at dawn.' The rest belonged to General Field-Marshal Cinque. He began by reminding the Hearsts of his statement on the last tape that the SLA awaited a good faith gesture, and would make their assessment of it. He went on: 'The Hearst empire has attempted to mislead the people and to deceive them by claiming to put forth a good faith gesture of $2 million. This amount is not at all a good faith gesture but rather is an act of throwing a few crumbs to the people, forcing them to fight over it among themselves.'

DeFreeze then catalogued the Hearsts' possessions and those of the Corporation: the silver mine, cattle ranches, timber land, family homes, interests in IBM, Safeway stores, Howard Hughes airlines, drug companies, paper companies and, of course, the publishing empire. There was even an accurate inventory of the Hillsborough house: ' . . . a collection of antique paintings, Chinese screens and Greek vases. Twenty-four vases each valued at $10,000; a collection of Oriental rugs given to him by his personal friend, the Shah of Iran . . . ' The business details could have been culled from reference books, but only Patty could have supplied the domestic details. The Hearst Foundation DeFreeze described as 'a front . . . a tax loophole for the Hearst fortune.'

The Foundation donates an estimated $3 million a year to established charities to maintain its legal status as a foundation. The $1.5 million proposed to be coming from the Foundation is nothing more than half of what that Foundation is legally required to donate annually in order to maintain its Foundation status . . .

In total, the Hearst empire, along with Mr and Mrs Hearst's personal wealth, does in fact go into the hundreds and hundreds of millions . . . Even if Mr Hearst were to give all that to the people, he could never pay the people back for the past losses of their children and freedom, nor for the current suffering they are now under.

Unrelentingly, the harsh, nasal, high-pitched voice went on to set out ten conditions to be met if the Hearst good-faith gesture were to be acceptable to the SLA. They added up to a demand that Hearst's $2 million be raised to $6 million, that the food distribution start within twenty-four hours, that the money be spent in a single month rather than as part of an on-going process, and that all who claimed to be in need, whether or not they were in possession of the welfare cards specified in the earlier communiqué, should be fed. In addition, a community group called the Western Addition Project Area Committee (WAPAC) was added to the approved list of observers and co-ordinators and designated chairman of the coalition with powers of veto over the coalition's activities. Participating organisations were encouraged to 'cry out for the millions of children of all races who are starving and dying now and not just cry out for the safety of only one human being who just happens to be the daughter of the enemy of the people.' If the demands were not met, said DeFreeze, Patty would be executed. He concluded by acknowledging that the press had identified him correctly, which led to a passage of bitter rhetoric which would not have shamed Malcolm X or even George Jackson:

> You do indeed know me. You have always known me. I'm that nigger you have hunted and feared night and day. I'm that nigger you have killed hundreds of my people in a vain hope of finding. I'm that nigger that is no longer just hunted, robbed and murdered. I'm that nigger that hunts you now.
> Yes, you know me. You know us all. You know me, I'm the wetback. You know me, I'm the gook, the broad, the servant, the spik.
> Yes indeed, you know us all, and we know you – the oppressor, murderer and robber. And you have hunted and

robbed and exploited us all. Now we are the hunters that will give you no rest. And we will not compromise the freedom of our children.

Then came the now-familiar signature: 'Death to the fascist insect that preys upon the life of the people.'

Hearst moved quickly. Somehow, with the aid of more than a thousand volunteers organised from a temporary office in the Hearst Corporation building, Ludlow Kramer contrived to beg, borrow and buy enough food to start the People In Need distribution within the twenty-four hours specified by DeFreeze.

Before daylight on Friday 22 February, lines began forming at the distribution centres which were advertised to open at noon. By ten o'clock the queue at the East Oakland centre, a Black Muslim bakery, was two blocks long and holding up the traffic.

An hour later the first two food trucks arrived, stacked with bags each containing a frozen turkey, a packet of savoury biscuits, a can of tomato juice, a box of biscuit mix, a quart of milk and a number of eggs. But the food trucks, like the rest of the traffic, couldn't get through the crowds. Frustrated by hours of waiting, men and women clambered aboard and started helping themselves. Bags were tossed down to friends. Turkeys flew through the air. A fist-fight broke out and a squad of police moved in to break it up. The lorries backed away, pursued by the eggs and tomatoes thrown by the unhappy crowds.

No more food arrived at the East Oakland centre and fighting started again, turning through the afternoon into an ugly riot. Rocks were hurled through shop fronts and at passing cars. A home-made firebomb was lobbed through the window of a hardware store. Shops in a nearby food market were broken into and looters emerged with armloads of food. A television cameraman was beaten and sent packing. By nightfall the Oakland police had made thirty-six arrests.

There was confusion at most other distribution centres too. Television and press reporters were chased away from the centre at Hunters Point, and that at East Palo Alto failed to open because no one had thought to arrange for the location, the

Tulip L. Jones Women's Club, to be unlocked. By the end of a disorderly day some 9000 people had received food compared with the 20,000 PIN had set out to accommodate. Kramer blamed logistical problems and the 'impatience' of the crowd.

Hearst's *Examiner* played down the chaos and ignored the Oakland violence altogether. Its reporters duly came up with pro-SLA quotes from food recipients: 'It's too bad his daughter had to be kidnapped for that filthy rich man to give food away' . . . 'More power to Cinque, I have seven kids and I can use the food' . . . 'I'm behind the SLA 101 per cent' . . . 'Do you know any black child they'd pay $2 million for?'

Hearst knew, meanwhile, that he must make a quick response to the demand for the $2 million to be raised to $6 million. His dilemma was evident: to refuse might be to sign Patty's death warrant, to comply was to open the door to what could become limitless extortion.

Earlier that week two things had happened which had made it even more difficult for him to surrender unconditionally. In Los Angeles, a group claiming to be a local unit of the SLA had issued a communiqué threatening the execution of Patty if security guards were not removed from the campus of Pepperdine University. While the communiqué was assumed to be bogus, it nevertheless showed that the threat of imitation feared by the authorities might indeed be materialising. Then, much more seriously, the editor of a Georgian paper, the *Atlanta Constitution*, was kidnapped and a ransom demand for $700,000 was sent to his family. Although he was released forty-eight hours later and an arrest followed, it seemed plain that the SLA's singularly successful tactics had found admirers beyond the borders of California. So Hearst could not submit, yet dared not refuse.

The manner in which he contrived to resolve this dilemma seemed at the time a shrewd one. He would tell the SLA he personally couldn't raise the money and was therefore handing the matter over to the more impersonal Hearst Corporation. The Corporation would agree to put up an immediate $2 million if Patty were released, to be followed by a further $2 million in

January 1975. The scheme appeared to have several advantages. The SLA might be convinced that the responsibility of bargaining for Patty had been transferred from the family to the Corporation and this would deprive them of a powerful emotional lever. If the cash offered by the Corporation was still far below the SLA's original demand, it was nevertheless twice the sum previously offered. So the Hearsts could reasonably claim to be making a realistic offer while simultaneously assuring the law-and-order lobby that they had turned down the SLA's full demands. It was a strategy of a shrewd employer locked in difficult negotiations with a truculent union, but hardly that of a man determined at all costs to get his daughter back.

Having secured the agreement of the Corporation, Hearst arranged to send his reply to the SLA through the now customary medium of a press and television conference at Hillsborough. On the afternoon of 22 February, as confusion seized the PIN centres and riots raged in Oakland, Randolph Hearst stepped up to the cluster of microphones on his front doorsteps and cleared his throat for the short exercise in brinkmanship which, quite unwittingly, was to give the Patty Hearst story a tragic new dimension.

Hearst said simply, 'The size of the latest demand of the Symbionese Liberation Army is far beyond my family capabilities. Therefore the matter is now out of my hands.'

And before reporters realised that that was all he had to say, Hearst turned on his heel, walked back into the house, and shut the door.

Then Charles Gould, Hearst's business partner, stepped forward to put the Corporation's offer: $2 million down now in return for Patty, and a legally binding agreement to provide $2 million more next January. And so that there should be no misunderstandings he went on, 'Neither the Hearst Corporation nor the Hearst Foundation are controlled by members of the Hearst family. No other funds will be committed by the Corporation or the Foundation under any circumstances.'

Gould's claim that the Hearst family didn't have full control of the business was to be queried later by Patty, who knew very

well that her father was chairman and his brother president.
But for the present the SLA had been given its answer.

As the ill-fated food distribution began, President Richard
Nixon sent his top law officers west to get a grip on the situation which was becoming something of an embarrassment to
his administration. The SLA had achieved the feat of winning
world-wide publicity for their charge that millions were hungry
in the richest state of the most powerful nation in the world,
a feat especially galling to an administration trying to show
that, Watergate and the crumbling economy notwithstanding,
the average American had never had it so good. So on 22 February, Attorney-General William Saxbe and FBI chief, Clarence
Kelley, flew into San Francisco from Washington 'to meet
terrorism head on', as Saxbe put it. 'Nothing,' added Kelley,
'will stand in the way of the SLA's apprehension,' meaning that
considerations of Patty's safety would no longer inhibit the
FBI's search and destroy mission – if indeed such considerations
had ever done so. The only real inhibition on the FBI was that
its employees didn't have a clue as to Patty's whereabouts.

Saxbe and Kelley had an additional reason for talking tough.
Charles Bates, the FBI investigator in charge of more than a
hundred agents on the case, had given his chiefs a confidential
briefing in the course of which he had speculated that Patty, far
from being a kidnap victim, had actually conspired with the
SLA to force her father to give away his fortune. The mere
notion that Hearst, the media and the FBI were all being taken
in by a conspiracy of juvenile radicals was in itself quite enough
to loosen whatever restraints federal agents and local police had
hitherto been working under.

Several factors had combined to feed Bates' suspicion that
Patty just might not be the innocent her parents believed her to
be. There was her unconventional life style – living with her
boyfriend and smoking pot. There was that extraordinary find
of cyanide-filled bullets in her apartment. There was the
apparent link between Nancy Ling Perry and Steven Weed in
Nancy's notebook. And there was the evidence of the tapes:

the hostile references to the FBI, contrasted with her understanding, almost sympathetic attitude towards her captors.

Pursuing the suspicion that Patty and Weed were secret radicals and co-conspirators, FBI agents subjected Weed to a gruelling interrogation about his past, culminating in a lie-detector test. They even demanded to know whether he had had sexual intercourse since Patty's disappearance, perhaps to test the sincerity of his relationship with her, though the relevance of the question is far from clear. They established that he had once shared a room with a prominent SDS activist and he told them, as he was later to tell curious newsmen, that his only connection with student radicalism was that he had once been drafted into his college's SDS football team to make up numbers for a key game with the Officers' Training Corps. His FBI interrogators were less amused than the journalists, but an exhaustive enquiry, during which almost every student acquainted with either Weed or Patty was relentlessly questioned, failed to turn up any evidence that either had ever been involved in the radical scene.

The FBI nevertheless continued to nurse its suspicion, which Bates passed on to Kelley and Saxbe. The story of Patty's complicity was also spread among media contacts. Because of the bizarre compact between the American media and the SLA, only foreign papers felt free to risk running the story and it was the London *Daily Telegraph* which first made the FBI's suspicions public. But while the American media felt obliged to lay off this aspect of the story, its private knowledge that the FBI was pursuing this line of enquiry effectively inhibited it from criticising the Bureau's increasingly hard line against the SLA.

Governor Reagan needed no public relations exercise to justify his gut reaction. On the eve of the second PIN food distribution he warned that all who accepted free food would be 'aiding and abetting lawlessness'. He hoped they would be rewarded by chronic food-poisoning – 'a dose of botulism'.

The Hearsts were now a lonely family, increasingly isolated from the conservative Republican law and order lobby to which they and their papers had given such long, unstinting support.

Ironically, if Randolph Hearst still had allies in his aim to
rescue his daughter they were no longer his political friends but
the coalition of radical and revolutionary groups involved in
PIN.

Hearst was now meeting and actively working with sections
of the community whose lives and concerns had never before
penetrated the invisible walls surrounding Hillsborough. A
strange thing happened as these new influences and alliances
made their mark. Very slowly, by the painful road of bitter
experience, Patty Hearst's father began to abandon conservative
simplicities and to turn towards liberalism.

After the confusion of the first food distribution, Kramer and
the PIN coalition struggled to ensure that there would be no
more riots or organisational fiascos. Further distributions were
postponed from 23 to 25 February, then to the 26th, then again
to the 28th. But while the time gained enabled the organisers to
stock up with food and transport, it also allowed time for
recriminations.

PIN's weakness was that while Kramer had nominal charge
of the way the Hearst money was spent, the SLA's terms meant
that real power lay with the participating organisations making
up the coalition, particularly WAPAC which the SLA had
designated as chairman with full powers of veto. Coalition meetings were often acrimonious as groups which had long competed
for community support brought in their obscure and often petty
rivalries. Each group wanted a full share of credit for successful
distributions, and each blamed its rivals for the failures. Meetings were tense and the power-struggles bitter. Kramer took
less than a week of it before going to Hearst to tell him he
wanted to quit. Hearst persuaded him to stay on the ground that
the collapse of the programme might cost Patty's life. But the
Washington politician was never more than a figurehead and a
cipher. It was the radicals who held real control.

PIN secured the use of a huge warehouse on the San Francisco waterfront. As the second distribution began, five days
late, scores of black and white volunteers in jeans and denim

jackets checked food into the trucks before they set out for the distribution centres. Armed guards were stationed at each entrance to discourage pilfering, but once the lorries had left the warehouse there was little control. One lorry load was hijacked, another misrouted, yet another spilt on the road after being inexpertly loaded. At one centre 25 per cent and at another 10 per cent of the food was reported stolen. At the end of the day there were conflicting claims on how many of the poor had been fed: Kramer said 28,000 and WAPAC chairman Arnold Townsend said 15,000. But this time at least there were no riots.

A third distribution followed on 5 March and a fourth on 8 March. Kramer claimed that PIN had spent most of Hearst's money and urged that Patty be released so that the first instalment of the Corporation's contribution could be released. The FBI raided two suspected SLA hideouts in the mountains north of San Francisco, but found nothing. Meanwhile, Colston Westbrook called a press conference on campus at Berkeley to complain that his BCA project at Vacaville had been 'sabotaged by white Maoists' and to name Willie Wolfe as a suspected SLA member.

Nearly two weeks had now passed without a word from Patty. A letter purportedly from the SLA was sent to three State Governors and a Senator, apparently picked at random, but it only repeated the warning Cinque had given on the last tape and contained no news whatever of Patty. Early in March, Randolph Hearst began telling friends he feared she was dead. On 3 March he went on television to broadcast an appeal to Patty to 'get the SLA to communicate – just so as we know you're OK'.

A week later, on 9 and 10 March, the SLA placed identical copies of a new tape in three San Francisco locations: one for KSAN radio in the ladies' lavatory at Foster's West restaurant, a second for KDIA radio in another Foster's West coffee house and a third for KPFA radio under a seat in a Metro cinema. Anonymous telephone calls told the stations where the tapes could be found.

After sixteen days agonised silence the Hearsts listened again to their daughter's voice. But her message brought them little comfort. It was preceded by a long tirade from Angela Atwood who introduced herself as 'Gelina, a General in the Symbionese Liberation Army'. She delivered the SLA's verdict on the PIN programme. It had 'shown contempt for the people' and had given them 'hog feed'. 'Instead of $70 worth of top-quality food, the people have gotten $8 worth of mediocre food. Instead of fresh meat, half the people received only chicken. Many stood in long, cold lines for only a bag of cabbages, while others stood in line and got nothing at all.'

As for the Hearst Corporation's offer, 'Hearst and the Hearst Corporation assumed that the SLA and the people were inexperienced in the area of corporate trickery, so they said that they would give $2 million upon Patricia Hearst's release and the rest in January 1975. However, the people have experienced such trickery too many times in the past to ever be fooled by it again . . . One thing above all, never trust the words of the enemy.'

There was much more, but it was Patty's message which provided the sensation. She spoke for eleven minutes in the bitter tones of a daughter who now believed she had been abandoned, beginning on a note of cruel sarcasm:

Mom, Dad, I received the message you broadcast last Sunday. It was good to hear from you after so much silence – and what you had to say sounded like you don't care if I ever get out of here. All you want is to hear from me sometimes. Your silence definitely jeopardised my safety because it allows the FBI to continue to attempt to find me and Governor Reagan to make antagonistic statements with no response from you.

I'm beginning to feel that the FBI would rather that I get killed. I'm telling you this now because I don't think the FBI will let any more words from me get through to the media.

I hear that people all around the country keep calling on the SLA to release me unharmed. But the SLA are not the ones who are harming me. It's the FBI, along with your indifference to the poor and your failure to deal with the people and the SLA in a meaningful, fair way.

I don't believe you're doing everything in your power. I

don't believe that you're doing anything at all. You said it was out of your hands. What you should have said was that you wash your hands of it.

I guess that you don't understand that it is not just the crimes of you and Mom personally that I am being held for but the crimes of the University of California Board of Regents and your voting record, Mom, when you were on that board. And also the crimes of the Hearst Corporation.

Dad, you can't put the responsibility for my status on the Hearst Corporation, but you seem to be ignoring the fact that you are the Chairman of the Board and Uncle Bill is President of the Hearst Corporation. I know that if anything happens to me it will be because your Corporation advisers and the FBI decided to protect their interests instead of my life.

I don't know who influenced you to not comply with the good faith gesture. I know that you could have done it the way the SLA asked. I mean, I know that we have enough money. But it seems to me that you told the FBI to do whatever they decide is necessary to destroy the SLA. But it's becoming true, Dad. I've heard the reports concerning the FBI investigation and interrogations. Governor Reagan's careless and antagonistic remarks and the attempts of Federal agencies to manoeuvre the news media, to mentally prepare the public for my death by calling for mass prayers and petitions to the SLA for my release.

From this I am forced to draw only one conclusion, that the FBI and other Federal agencies want me to die. I no longer seem to have any importance as a human being; rather, I have become all-important as a political pivot-point for certain Right-wing elements and I can only be used successfully by these people if I am killed.

As for the constant reassurances by the FBI that my safety is their primary concern, I can only say that the FBI has never been famous for its concern for the safety of hostages and from what I've seen so far this case is no different.

Whether consciously or not, the news media has been assisting the FBI in its now overt attempts to set me up for execution. It has done this primarily in two ways.

First, by promoting a public image of my father as a bereaved parent who has done all he can do to meet the demands of his daughter's kidnappers and who now awaits her supposedly long overdue release. In fact, the SLA demands have not even been approximated and they have made it very clear that until the good faith gesture is completed, negotiations for my release will not begin.

Second, the media, with co-operation from my parents, has created a public image of me as a helpless, innocent girl who was supposedly abducted by two terrible blacks, escaped convicts. I am a strong woman and I resent being used in this way.

I have been hearing reports about the food programme. So far it sounds like you and your advisers have managed to turn it into a real disaster. I heard only 15,000 people received food in the first two weeks and that each of them received only about $8 worth. It sounds like most of the food is of low quality. No one received any beef or lamb, and it certainly didn't sound like the kind of food our family is used to eating.

The SLA wanted this programme to be over in one month. They wanted each person to get $70 worth of good food all at once. If you'd just done what the SLA wanted for the food programme the month would almost be over and I would be ready to get out of here.

What you've done is tell People In Need to set up this programme where people get almost an $8 bag of food, so it's being stretched out and it's a really discouraging thing for people who need food.

Dad, I know that you got most of the food *donated* for People In Need. And you have put very little money at all into the programme.

Mom, I can't believe that you agree with the 'out of my hands' stand that Dad has taken. I just wish that you could be stronger and pull yourself together from all these emotional outbursts and see if you can persuade Dad to listen to you and the rest of the family.

Mom, you've got to stand up and speak for yourself. You seem to be allowing other people to make your decisions. Your statements, if I can call them that, have given the FBI the go-ahead to kill me. I wish God would touch your heart and get you to do something concrete to help me. I wish I knew what the rest of the family was thinking and saying. It's hard to believe that my sisters and cousins aren't saying anything.

If it had been you, Mom, or you, Dad, who had been kidnapped instead of me, I know that I and the rest of the family and your friends would do anything to get you back. It could have been one of you and how would you feel if you had been written off the way I seem to have been.

I'm starting to think that no one is concerned about me any more. I wish that I could hear from the rest of the family. I'd like to hear what my sisters have to say about Dad's decision about not to comply with the terms of the good faith gesture.

Steven, what do you have to say? Willy, [William Randolph Hearst, Patty's cousin] I know you really care about what happens to me. Make Dad let you talk. You can't be silent.

Everyone who hears this tape, I hope you will believe me and not think that I've been brainwashed or tortured into saying this. Please listen to me because I'm speaking honestly and from the heart.

In the last week, it's become obvious to the SLA and all hungry people and to me that my father is not even attempting to show a gesture of good faith. I guess that everybody knows that is why there's been no further word from the SLA about negotiating for my release.

In the last few days members of the Federation have spoken with me. They have given me some newspaper reports to read about the current practices of psycho-surgery and the daily use of drugs and tranquilisers in prisons throughout the country. I have also been given some journal commentaries about kinds of conditions that exist in prisons in general and in the adjustment centre at San Quentin in particular.

Members of the Federation have also given me a choice of books to read. I have been reading a book by George Jackson called *Blood in My Eye*. I'm starting to understand what he means when he talks about fascism in America. Joseph Remiro and Russell Little, the two men in San Quentin, haven't come to trial yet and already they are being held in strip cells on Death Row. It's really hard to believe that such an odious violation of the constitution is taking place, but it's true.

How can people think that these men can get a fair trial? Can there be any doubt in people's mind as to what the verdict will be?

Members of the Federation are studying intelligence reports gathered by the SLA on the activities of the FBI. These, combined with discussions the members of the Federation have had with me and my own observations of the way my father's been conducting himself, have made me afraid because I realise that the plans are coming from the FBI and the Attorney-General's office in Washington to execute the two men in San Quentin, or if that cannot be swiftly accomplished, to execute me by seeing to it that even if I am released I will not get home alive. Or by attempting to raid this place where I am being held and then discredit the SLA by saying that they were the ones who killed me.

Because of these dangers I have been transferred to a special security unit of the SLA combat forces, where I am being held in protective custody.

I have been issued with a 12-gauge riot shotgun and I have been receiving instructions on how to use it.

While I have no access to ammunition, in the event of an attack by the FBI I have been told that I will be given an issue of cyanide buckshot in order to protect myself, because it is the Federation's opinion and my own from observation that if the FBI does rush in they will obviously be doing it against the wishes of my family and in total disregard for my safety. In fact they would be doing it to murder me.

Under international codes of war I am allowed to communicate with members of my family and, because of the scope of this incident, to the public as well. However, I should tell you that the practice of allowing me to communicate with you will not continue until the SLA hears from the two men in San Quentin. They want to hear what the two men have to say in a live nationwide broadcast so they can hear all the conditions of their confinement.

I really want to get out of here and I really want to get home alive. I am appealing to the public and asking them not to assist the FBI in their investigation. Doing so is simply helping them to dig my grave.

I ask those people who say they pray for me and those who sign petitions to the SLA for my safe release to redirect their energies into opposing the FBI's brutal attempts to murder me and the two men in San Quentin.

I no longer fear the SLA because they are not the ones who want me to die. The SLA wants to feed the people and assure safety and justice for the two men at San Quentin.

I realise now it is the FBI who wants to murder me. Only the FBI and certain people in the government stand to gain anything by my death.

There Patty's voice broke off. It was an astonishing and mystifying outburst. The bitter insistence that 'I know you have enough money', the growing fear that she was being 'set up for execution', the conviction that she had been abandoned by her family and her fiancé, her concern for Little and Remiro, her apparent assumption of the justice of her captors' cause and finally her chilling statement that she had been armed with a shotgun and was receiving instructions on how to use it – all this made a nonsense of the public image of a poor, helpless, innocent young girl snatched from the bosom of a loving family and held a terrorised captive by militant blacks and crazed revolutionaries. After five weeks of captivity, something was beginning to happen to Patty Hearst.

There was another message on the end of the tape – a message from someone who had once, like Patty, exemplified the All-American girl until something had happened to change her. The voice was Mizmoon's and she was urging 'comrade sisters and freedom fighters' to 'turn your rage towards the enemy in a direct line down the sights of your guns'.

The tape marked a watershed in the puzzling story of Patty Hearst. The first result was that the other SLA captive, the press, decided it was time to make a break for freedom. They would do the SLA's bidding to protect an innocent kidnap victim but not for one who seemed now to have some sympathy for her captors. Perhaps it was true, as the FBI had hinted, that Patty had been party to a giant hoax. Perhaps they had all been taken in.

So on the morning of 10 March, the *Oakland Tribune* announced that it would no longer publish SLA communiqués in full. Other editors followed suit, some calling Hearst to explain or make their excuses. 'We all want to see Patty come home,' said one, 'but we can't go on like this. From now on we'll be giving the SLA only the space they merit.'

Hearst's response was that of a journalist who knows the big story has yet to break: 'That's still going to be an awful lot of space.'

5 Conversion

On that dramatic evening of 4 February 1974, in a quiet side street half a dozen blocks from Patty's apartment, the SLA's hijacked Chevrolet Impala, with Patty's bruised and bleeding body slumped in the boot, pulled up behind Camilla Hall's Volkswagen. Patty was transferred to the Volkswagen and driven off to the SLA's hideout.

It isn't clear where she was first taken. The SLA seems to have kept on the move, without a permanent base, for a month or so after the abortive attempt by Nancy to fire the Concord house and 'melt away the fingerprints'. Since Camilla, on the night of the kidnapping, was the only member of the group who had not yet gone underground and disappeared, it may well have been to her apartment on Francisco Street that Patty was taken. There, or wherever it was they kept her, her scrapes and bruises were cleaned up and for a time her hands were tied, her eyes blindfolded and her mouth gagged. But her captors seem to have decided quickly that blindfolds and gags were unnecessary. A week after her abduction the prisoner sent her parents the message that she was being well treated, that her kidnappers were not 'nuts' and their demands should be met. So far it seemed to follow the pattern of a standard kidnapping.

An immediate practical problem for the SLA was lack of money. Those who had been working had quit their jobs without notice in the panic following the arrest of Little and Remiro. Now they had nine mouths to feed and a revolution to make. So on 12 February – the day KPFA radio received Patty's first tape – Emily Harris wrote to a former schoolfriend in Indiana:

Bill and I are both better than ever and into some really interesting things. We have moved but have no permanent address yet. I need to ask your help on doing a favor. We need to have the enclosed message delivered to Bill's mother. She can't receive it in the mail for reasons which I will have to explain later, so if you could just drop it by in person as soon as possible. Thank you for helping!

Things are moving very fast around here and our interest in the prisons has carried us into many different areas. I will write more soon but for now I am anxious to get this in the mail so Bill's Mom will get it soon. She should not be too surprised so don't worry about that. Love to you all, Emily.

The friend, wondering a little at the air of mystery but not dreaming to connect Emily with the events then in the newspaper headlines, duly delivered Bill's message to Mrs Harris. It asked her to send a cheque for $1500 for 'food and certain necessities', Bill's situation being 'critical due to lack of mobility'. The cheque was to be sent in an enclosed stamped and addressed envelope via a friend, Janet Cooper, to a post office box number in Santa Clara. Janet Cooper was a Venceremos activist who was to make a second appearance later in the SLA story, ultimately being called to testify before a Federal grand jury.

On 19 February Mrs Harris sent off an instalment of $250 in the envelope addressed to Janet Cooper, and heard nothing more from her son.

Meanwhile Emily's own father, Frederick Schwartz, was trying to make sense of the letter his daughter had sent him a few days earlier telling of her love for a beautiful black man and hinting at a mysterious change in her life style. When he heard of the Patty Hearst kidnapping he had a 'gut feeling' that Emily and her friends were involved. Unable to make contact by ringing her apartment, he went to his local FBI office in Chicago. Within two days of the kidnapping, the FBI was checking out the background of Emily Harris, her husband, and the girl who had been sharing their apartment, Angela Atwood – whose husband, Gary Atwood, was of course named on a library ticket found a month earlier in the Concord house.

More important, since Patty may well have been kept at her apartment, the FBI was quickly on to Camilla Hall – though not quite as soon as it might have been. While Emily was writing home for money, Camilla was raising funds by selling her Volkswagen to a used car dealer. What she didn't know was that Patty's neighbours had given the FBI a description of the car after spotting its role as look-out vehicle during the kidnapping. It was the most wanted car in San Francisco. Ironically, the dealer resold the car to a secretary who worked in the San Francisco office of the FBI and as police scoured the city for it, the unsuspecting new owner drove to work each day and parked right outside FBI headquarters. It was ten days before it was noticed, and another day before the FBI eliminated the alarming possibility that it had an SLA member within its own ranks. But in the end, tracing back the car's registration, they arrived at Camilla Hall's name and discovered she had abandoned her apartment only a day or two earlier, on 19 February.

The car dealer's cheque for $1500, made out in her name, was traced to the Central Bank on Shattuck Avenue, Berkeley, where Camilla had paid it in on 15 February. Here the FBI stumbled on another lead. Running through the bank's list of depositors they came across the name of Nancy Ling Perry, whose membership of the SLA was by now public knowledge.

It so happened that the bank stood across the street from the Berkeley FBI office. It would have been a simple operation to keep it under observation or to post agents inside. But the FBI decided it wasn't worth doing so, and didn't even tell the Oakland police department of their discovery so that *they* could stake it out. Instead, they relied on a loose arrangement with bank staff that if either of the SLA suspects showed up again, the FBI would be informed.

On 1 March, only four days after the Bureau had uncovered her account, Camilla Hall walked into the bank and withdrew her $1500. Through what the bank described laconically as 'a mix-up' the clerk failed to notify the FBI or the police. Had the bank been staked out and Camilla Hall followed, it is virtually certain she would have led investigators to the apartment where Patty was being held. Instead, the police and the 'feds' were left to their mutual recriminations. Neither agency ever had as good a chance again of locating Patty and attempting a rescue.

Some time in February or early March, one of the SLA members rented the tiny apartment which was to become the group's 'safe house' – and the birthplace of 'Tania'.

Golden Gate Avenue, San Francisco, is a main thoroughfare, at the downtown end of which stands FBI headquarters. Number 1827 is at the seedier end. In apartment 6, a bright, sunny lounge looks out over the avenue. Apart from a bathroom and a kitchen, it is the apartment's only room. A folding double-bed built into the wall makes it a dual purpose bed-sitting-room. Here in this tiny home Patty was to spend eight or nine incredible weeks with Donald DeFreeze, the Harrises, Willie Wolfe, Angela, Mizmoon, Camilla and Nancy. Chris Thompson had quit the group at least three months earlier and so it seems had Thero Wheeler, rather more recently. So one black 'field-marshal', two white lieutenants, five girl-soldiers and a captive shared an extraordinary family life together in a single cramped room. By day they listened to soul music and rock, watched television, read about themselves in the newspapers, cooked exotic dishes, drank canned beer and plum wine and talked, talked, talked about the revolution. At night they slept, some on the bed, others on the floor, in free and varying combinations.

Patty cannot help but have been deeply involved in the extravagant communal life of her captors. She wasn't shut up in a cell and couldn't be excluded from their conversation, music, food, comradeship. Forced to share many of the practicalities of life with them, she also came to share their greatest fear: that the FBI would somehow find them and shoot its way in. She probably watched the television news film of the FBI bursting into the suspected SLA hideout in Oakland – the incident referred to in the second of her taped messages. Perhaps, too, after watching her father announce on the steps at Hillsborough that the SLA's demands were 'out of my hands' she came to believe, because of her deep sense of having been betrayed and abandoned, the taunts of her SLA captors which implied that the hard head of Hearst the capitalist would overrule the soft heart of Hearst the father.

Steven Weed had never known Patty read a political book in all the months they lived together, but she started reading now. One of the books the SLA gave her was George Jackson's *Blood in My Eye*, a brilliant and passionate plea for America's blacks and underprivileged. On the very first page she would have seen among Jackson's list of 'right-wing traditionalists' and 'fascists' the name Hearst.

During those weeks in captivity Patty discovered, as other kidnap victims before her had discovered, that her captors were human beings – not the swarthy, celluloid terrorists of B-features and the public imagination but lively, intelligent and passionate people of her own age and, in some cases, her own background. They laughed, played around, made love. And they had a cause which they pursued with a strength of conviction she had never encountered before. They really *did* want to feed the hungry and were prepared to *do* something about it. Maybe they were wrong – but was her millionaire father and his effortlessly luxurious life-style right or defensible?

Perhaps Patty's experience was not altogether dissimilar to that of another rich young woman who, back in 1970, had been drawn into a revolutionary Weatherman commune, and had written later: 'It struck me . . . that they were a family. A big, very tight family. I wanted to be part of that. People were touching each other. Women together, men together. They were beautifully free. I felt that they were experiencing a whole new life-style that I really hadn't begun to understand. They were so full of life and energy and determination and love.'

So, conscious perhaps of previously undiscovered dimensions to life, with her news of the outside world and of her father's actions filtered through her captors' carefully selective prism, and with her personal safety and eventual fate becoming identified more strongly each day with that of her room-mates, Patty began to adjust to her life as a prisoner. Gradually the guard on her was relaxed until, still technically a prisoner, she was given a shotgun and shown how to use it against the SLA's enemies, who had now come to seem her enemies too.

Outside the tiny apartment which the SLA fantasised as the cradle of the American Revolution, outside in the real world, the American Left struggled to come to terms with what had happened.

The New Left had languished in a broody silence for three years. The reforms once passionately worked for had receded beyond sight, the revolution once dreamed of had been supplanted by the age of Richard Nixon. All over the country the veteran activists of the sixties, America's mainly white, middle-class intelligentsia, were now making their mark in the respectable worlds of teaching, journalism and law. Some were political drop-outs; others still pursued their dreams, but without illusions, knowing the golden year of 1968 would never return.

Suddenly this generation of residual revolutionaries, the old New Left, found themselves upstaged by a tiny band of bizarre desperados who broke all the ideological rules but, incredibly, succeeded in holding the mighty American press captive for a month while forcing a multi-millionaire to disgorge his fortune to feed the poor and needy. Arguably the SLA had achieved more in weeks than the New Left had achieved in a decade.

The response of the revolutionary student movement was one of anger tinged with envy: anger because the SLA's élitist adventurism threatened what could be an unprecedented crackdown on all dissent, and envy at the group's outrageous nerve and success.

'I didn't think we had it in us,' wrote a veteran of many Berkeley protests. 'I don't mean I approve of the SLA, but I always thought the American Left was just not capable of pulling off such well-planned, well-executed urban guerrilla actions.' Jerry Rubin, hero of the Chicago Conspiracy trial, demon-

strated a similar reluctant admiration: 'The incredible fanati-
cism expressed in a willingness to kill and die is a completely
new development in America on the Left . . . This is no
anarchistic, dope-smoking, careless group of hippies . . . These
are angry, dedicated, fanatical people. How many years do you
suppose they have worked together to establish ideology, cadre,
organisation, hideout places and weaponry like cyanide bullets?'
    Rubin offered some advice to the SLA – advice which, as
events turned out, proved to be particularly prescient.

> If you kill Patricia Hearst, you will be outraging human
> beings everywhere. You will start off a Right-wing crack-
> down – 'Find the SLA!' – that will endanger the very people
> you are fighting for. You will destroy the moral credibility
> of the Left.
> Fight for all you can get for the people from your tem-
> porary position of power-leverage, and then release Patricia
> unharmed. Treat her with such love and understanding that
> she comes away from you respecting and digging you. Win
> her over as an ally to your cause. Under no circumstances
> harm her. That would be a crime outside the boundaries of
> any revolutionary morality.

Beyond the student Left, the response of established socialist
groups and their journals was more unequivocally critical.
Ramparts thought the SLA no more revolutionary than a street
gang, and the Maoist *Guardian* dismissed it as 'nothing more
than a band of strong-arm fundraisers on behalf of public
charity'. The San Francisco Socialist Coalition thought the SLA
meant well but was on a wrong-headed and dangerous tack:

> It is wrong to categorize them as simply a bunch of mis-
> guided, crazy individuals acting in a fantasy world of their
> own making. They say that they are committed revolu-
> tionaires. Their actions have certainly dramatized that com-
> mitment . . . The tragedy of the SLA is that they are living
> out the rhetoric that was once so popular among sections of
> the New Left. We think that it is both frustration with the

ineffectiveness of the anti-imperialist socialist movement and outrage at the injustices of our society which propel groups like the SLA to the self-destructive, dead-end acts they have committed. They have become too impatient with the long and difficult work of building a mass movement. The SLA has decided that the time is ripe for armed combat and that they are 'the army of the people'. They couldn't be more wrong.

The SLA claims it speaks 'for the people'. This heady assertion flies in the face of the reality of most people's reaction to the Foster slaying and the Hearst kidnapping. The nature of the SLA's actions guarantee that the masses of people have no say at all about the course of the SLA's decisions. It reduces people to passive spectators, and further reinforces the view that the Left is a bunch of wild-eyed adventurers, removed from ordinary life, living in a fantasy world of revolution, guns and romantic acts.

The chorus of condemnation swelled with contributions from Huey Newton and the Black Panthers, Angela Davis and the Communist Party, Cesar Chavez, Jane Fonda, Tom Hayden, and scores of lesser luminaries. Even organisations and individuals once associated with SLA members now denounced them. Venceremos called them 'counter-revolutionary', and Dan Siegel, a radical lawyer who acted for members of the Peking House commune, described the SLA as 'a threat and a setback, giving a picture of the Left as wanton, crazy killers'. An anonymous group claiming to be 'former SLA members' drafted SLA-type communiqués condemning the tactics of terrorism. Even 'Popeye' Jackson, leader of the United Prisoners Union and only months earlier a close associate of Mizmoon, Camilla and other SLA members, now disparaged his old friends: 'When they talk about violent revolution, they're living in a dream world! We don't have no nuclear weapons, we don't have no jets, we can't buy one tank. How we gonna have a revolution? We have to educate the people first.'

To all this, 'General Gelina' made scornful response in her contribution to the taped communiqué of 9 March. Criticisms of the SLA, she said, came from leaders who were either 'cowards afraid of revolutionary violence because it is a direct threat to their personal security', or 'opportunists who have personal gains in allowing the enemy to enslave or oppress and tranquilize the people . . . '

It has been claimed that we are destroying the Left, but in truth an unarmed and non-fighting Left is doomed – as the people of Chile can sadly testify . . .

The dream, and indeed it is a dream, of this reactionary leadership is that the enemy corporate state will willingly give the stolen riches of the earth back to the people and that this will be accomplished through compromising talk and empty words.

In reality, the enemy state forces the people to buy back the goods that the people themselves have produced at the price of blood. To this, our bullets scream loudly. The enemy's bloodthirsty greed will be destroyed by the growing spirit of the people and their thirst for freedom.

The actions of the SLA are based on a clear understanding and analysis of the enemy and its actions against the lives and freedom of the people.

We call upon the people to judge for themselves whether our tactics of waging struggle are correct or incorrect in fighting the enemy by any means necessary.

With television cameras watching his every move and press notebooks recording his every word, Randolph Hearst struggled to hold a course which would appease his daughter's kidnappers without resort to the kind of unconditional surrender and abject capitulation which Saxbe, Kelley and Reagan feared. So while giving away his money in an unprecedented fashion, he also found it necessary to tell the SLA that enough was enough, that the limits had been reached, and further concessions were out of his hands. It never occurred to Hearst, until the tapes began to make it plain, that Patty would misread his situation and conclude that she was being abandoned.

One of the tragic ironies of the whole extraordinary story is that at the very time Patty's conviction took root that her family were not doing all they could for her, Randolph Hearst was beginning a series of secret negotiations with friends and close associates of the SLA. And just as his daughter was beginning to absorb something of the SLA's radical perspectives on the problems of the poor and oppressed, so too was Randolph Hearst. Patty's tutors were the SLA on the run: Randolph's were the SLA behind bars.

The man who conceived the bold idea of bringing Hearst face to face with SLA contacts was a fifty-year-old staff psychiatrist at Vacaville prison named Wesley Hiler. Hiler's patients included several BCA and Unisight members, among them Albert Taylor, the Polar Bear Party prisoner, whose letters to Nancy Ling Perry had been found half-burned in the Concord House. Taylor, now twenty-two, had committed six murders by the time he was nineteen, but in the course of a therapy session with Hiler he criticised the SLA for murdering Foster. Hiler learned that Taylor had been a member of Unisight – the founding group which had become the SLA.

Another of Hiler's patients was a black prisoner known as Joe K. Joe also told the psychiatrist that he had been active in Unisight but dropped out because 'there were radicals coming to the meetings to recruit future parolees to do political assassinations'.

After the Hearst kidnapping, Hiler made it his business to learn all he could about the SLA from these and other sources. Independently, Taylor and Joe K. both told him that the real leader of the SLA was Clifford 'Death Row' Jefferson, who was in the twenty-eighth year of his life sentence.

Jefferson had been questioned by prison officials as one of the more influential prisoners on Nancy Ling Perry's visiting list. He told them little, and the officials concluded that if Jefferson had ever had a leadership role in the group, it was probably over by now. But Taylor and Joe K. insisted to Hiler that Jefferson was still the leader with authority over the actions of DeFreeze and his 'combat unit'. Hiler arranged to see Jefferson in nearby Folsom jail.

The psychiatrist quickly built up a relationship of trust with the legendary veteran revolutionary. Hiler decided he was a frustrated idealist, consumed by hostility towards the ruling class but troubled at the prospect of innocents suffering through revolutionary violence. Whether Jefferson was the formal leader or simply a father-figure of the SLA, Hiler decided that he might have the authority to secure Patty's release.

At 1.30 pm on Thursday 21 February, seventeen days after the kidnapping and the day the SLA announced its angry rejection of Hearst's $2 million plan, Joe Remiro and Russell Little, on 'Death Row' at San Quentin, were astonished to be told by their guard that there was a phone call for them from their old friend Clifford Jefferson. Phone calls from anyone were a rare privilege: a call from another inmate was unheard of. Jefferson explained that he had persuaded prison chief Raymond Procunier to allow the call, and also to allow a meeting of the three prisoners at midnight that night to discuss their own situation and that of Patty Hearst.

At 10.30 pm three guards handcuffed Little and Remiro and led them outside the prison walls to a waiting car. They were driven the short distance to Folsom jail, where they were shown into an office near the visitors' waiting-room. Then Jefferson was brought in, accompanied by Procunier and other officials whom Little and Remiro assumed to be FBI agents. In these inauspicious circumstances, the three prisoners began to thrash out a tentative plan to help the SLA and get Patty released.

After two hours, they had agreed a four-point plan. First, capitalising on the unprecedented success of their comrades in holding the media captive, they demanded facilities for a press conference to 'tell the truth' about conditions in San Quentin. Second, they wanted the Little and Remiro trial to take place outside California, perhaps even outside the United States, since 'the speculative, biased, misinformative campaign' that they claimed had been waged against them made a fair trial virtually impossible. Third, they wanted Hearst to find more cash, and finally they wanted some sort of amnesty for the kidnappers. If these conditions were fulfilled, they would 'recommend' Patty's release.

This amounted to even steeper demands than the SLA had made in their communiqués. The plan was still-born. Procunier concluded that Jefferson had no real influence with the SLA and he didn't even consider it worthwhile to put the plan to Hearst. The press conference proposal was scotched by the prisoners' own defence lawyers who were afraid they would indiscreetly jeopardise their cases. Little and Remiro were transferred two days later from San Quentin to Alameda County jail, from which they managed to smuggle out a letter to KPFA radio telling of their midnight meeting with Jefferson and the FBI (who promptly denied being present) and complaining that they were being mistreated by prison authorities in the hope that the SLA would show its hand in an ill-judged act of retaliation. The letter also accused Saxbe and Kelley of wanting Patty Hearst to be killed, the better to discredit the SLA in the eyes of the nation's oppressed. The door, it seemed, was firmly slammed shut against an initiative from that quarter.

Wesley Hiler tried nevertheless to prise it open again. He had another meeting with Jefferson on 8 March, the day after KPFA received and broadcast the Little-Remiro letter. Jefferson made it clear that his prime concern was the safety of the kidnappers. He didn't want the SLA defeated, either by being wiped out themselves in a shoot-out or by allowing Patty to be killed, thereby forfeiting the popular support he believed them to be winning. And he feared the ultimate defeat: a negotiated release for Patty, followed by the police killing of her kidnappers and a wave of oppression against the entire Left.

Hiler asked him bluntly whether he was in a position to order Patty's release if the right terms could be agreed. Was he the leader of the SLA? Jefferson replied that the SLA wasn't like that. It wasn't a tightly disciplined army, and commands, from whatever quarter, were not automatically obeyed. Leadership relied on persuasion and was collective and democratic. Before deciding to follow a certain course of action, the SLA would debate it endlessly and eventually, if necessary, take a vote on it. Hiler got the impression that the murder of Foster had been decided by just such a vote after an inconclusive debate.

Clearly Jefferson couldn't order Patty's release. But Hiler

clung to his conviction that despite the earlier debacle 'the old man of the troops' could wield a powerful influence if he could be persuaded that Patty's release was in the SLA's interests. Tentatively he put to Jefferson the outline of a simple plan: the SLA would release Patty in return for some form of guaranteed immunity from prosecution, perhaps in the form of a flight to Cuba.

Jefferson responded hopefully by saying he'd like to meet Hearst. Hiler said he'd try to arrange it. As he explained later, 'the SLA had a lot of paranoid ideas about what the capitalists were like, and Hearst must have had a lot of negative ideas about what SLA members are like'. He had an image of Randolph Hearst and 'Death Row' Jeff 'talking sort of with tears in their eyes, embracing and realising each was a good person after all'.

Next day Patty's tape bitterly criticising PIN and her parents hit the headlines. Hiler couldn't get in touch with Hearst.

On 10 March the psychiatrist saw the Rev Cecil Williams, who had established a good relationship with Hearst in the course of his work for PIN. Williams often acted as a mediator between authority and the radical underground and he enthusiastically agreed to play impresario in bringing Hearst and Jefferson together. A call was put through to Hearst and a planning meeting arranged for that same evening in a conference room at the Hilton Hotel.

Hearst arrived with his wife and their nephew, William Randolph Hearst III. Hiler and Williams were the only others present. Hiler told Hearst that he thought Jefferson was either the leader or part of the collective leadership of the SLA. He was, said the psychiatrist, a frustrated idealist with sound, basic humanitarian instincts. If Hearst approached him in an understanding way, joining with him in the search for a way to save the lives of the combat unit as well as Patty, it was possible Jeff might get something moving.

Hearst showed interest, but wanted a lawyer present at the meeting. He didn't want to make promises he wouldn't be allowed to keep. Hiler and Williams suggested Vincent Hallinan, a veteran leftist whom Hiler had already cleared with

Jefferson. A call was put through on the spot and Hallinan not only agreed to do it but confirmed to Hearst that, according to his private sources, Jefferson was leader of the SLA and could deliver whatever he promised.

Hearst also agreed to make a public statement supporting the earlier demand by Little and Remiro for a press conference and a television appearance. If the jailed couple's lawyers were the stumbling-block, said Hearst, Little and Remiro could fire them and he would hire Hallinan to defend them. A pre-recorded TV appearance should pose no problems since Hallinan or the current defence lawyers could edit out anything which might prove prejudicial at their trial.

Finally a call was put through to the prison system chief to request an early meeting with Jefferson. To Hiler's astonishment, Procunier at first angrily refused. It would be a waste of time, he insisted: Jefferson might once have been associated with the SLA but he was sure he wasn't any longer the leader. Procunier thought he had quarrelled with DeFreeze and had long since lost whatever influence he had ever had on the group. But Hearst insisted it was worth a try. Procunier eventually agreed to a meeting next day.

Hiler also put to Procunier a fallback plan for a more bizarre meeting between Mrs Hearst and Albert Taylor. The two, he thought, had a lot in common, and if Catherine Hearst could get through to Taylor she might find a way of making contact with Nancy Ling Perry. But that was too much for Procunier. He refused, and wouldn't be budged.

Next morning Randolph Hearst drove from Hillsborough to Folsom and, with Vincent Hallinan, was shown into 'Death Row' Jeff's cell. They were left alone for an hour: the fifty-two-year-old multi-millionaire who had lost a daughter, the forty-eight-year-old lifer who had lost a dozen comrades, and a radical lawyer whose contempt for the conservative politics of the Hearst press was matched only by his distaste for the violence of the SLA.

Jefferson was later to tell Hiler he liked Hearst, finding him a sincere man who seemed to understand the SLA's position. Hearst was genuinely impressed with Jefferson. He told Cecil

Williams he had wanted to stay right there with him in the cell. As the meeting ended, the two men embraced.

That afternoon Hearst told a press conference on the steps at Hillsborough that Little and Remiro should be given TV time to 'air their views' and that he had hired Vincent Hallinan to make out a case to that effect before the courts. He also promised a revamping of the PIN programme and in effect apologised to the SLA for not following their original demands more closely. Observers were puzzled as to why, so soon after the 'out of my hands' speech, his tone should now be so conciliatory.

But events over the next few days were not propitious for the Hearsts. First, Steven Weed gave a television interview in which he said bluntly that he didn't trust the FBI and that neither he nor Patty shared the Hearst family's politics. Then WAPAC, the leading community group in the coalition observing and co-ordinating the PIN programme, issued a report that was bitterly critical of Kramer's organisation of the food distribution and of the quality of food being given away. Then, with extraordinarily ill-judged timing, Governor Reagan announced that Catherine Hearst had accepted re-appointment to a further fifteen-year term on the University of California Board of Regents, the very position which had led to the SLA describing her as an 'enemy of the people'. While this was being interpreted by observers as a hard-line message to the SLA, there was another much-publicised but non-political kidnapping, this time of a six-year-old boy. Although he was released within twelve hours when his father couldn't meet the $100,000 ransom, the event inevitably served to harden public opinion against policies of leniency or compromise towards kidnappers. Then finally, Little and Remiro refused to change lawyers, which made for serious complications in the Hearst-Jefferson initiative, since Jefferson was reluctant to act over their heads and they were equally reluctant to act without their lawyers' blessing.

Nevertheless, on 17 March, six days after their first meeting, Hearst again saw Jefferson who told Hearst that an appeal from him alone might not carry much weight with the SLA. A

renewed effort would have to be made to secure the co-operation of Little and Remiro. Hearst promptly persuaded prison
chief Procunier to allow Jefferson to put through another call to
the two SLA inmates, their first contact since the abortive
midnight meeting three weeks earlier. Jefferson was left alone
to make the call but, unknown to him, Hearst and a prison
officer listened in through a tapping device in the next room.
The conversation confirmed that Jefferson carried no more than
a marginal authority, but it also confirmed his sincerity. He
made strenuous efforts to assure a sceptical Little and Remiro
that Hearst was a good guy who wouldn't promise what he
couldn't persuade the FBI and the Attorney-General to deliver.
But the conversation ended inconclusively. The prison officer
listening in with Hearst ventured the opinion that the SLA
couple were 'hostile fanatics and smart alecs' who, if given a TV
appearance, would 'come out with a lot of garbage'.

After the meeting Hearst drove into San Francisco to see
Judge Sam Hall who was dealing with Hallinan's application
for the Little and Remiro TV appearance. The judge wouldn't
reveal his decision. But next day he made it clear that the
appearance would not be allowed since it would prejudice a
fair trial and set an undesirable precedent. The first precondi-
tion of an initiative from Jefferson had collapsed.

Hearst's immediate concern was to make it clear to Patty
that, if efforts to get her out seemed to be falling apart, it was
not through lack of effort on his part. In a televised message
to her he said, 'Just hang in there, we're doing everything
we can and we've got a lot of people working on it. I love
you and want you back, and Catherine wants you back, we
all do, the whole family wants you back.' And he told the press,
'I can understand her irritation, I can understand the fact that
she wants us to do more, but I think we've tried everything we
could.' And he wasn't going to accept Judge Hall's ruling as
final. 'I'm going to keep asking the people that have the
authority to let them do it. If they say no they say no, but I'm
going to keep on asking . . . I can see how people are afraid of
setting a precedent. On the other hand, I think this whole case is
a precedent.'

Then, for the first time, Randolph Hearst talked publicly about the SLA's aims and methods. And the criticism he levelled was not that of his conservative associates but rather that of typical liberals and the Left. The SLA, he charged, was obscuring its worthy objectives by focusing attention on its means rather than its ends.

We're in a position here of looking at the fellow who threw the brick through a window, hoping you'd look inside to see what was there. Instead, everybody is looking at the man who threw the brick.

They're trying to make a political statement and they've gone to the extreme of capturing a child of someone who's in the media business, hoping to point up a great many of the injustices that are existing in our country today. But what's happening is that, instead of looking at those injustices, instead of looking at our school systems, instead of realising there are people who need to be fed, instead of realising that the Indians are in trouble, instead of realising that people in this country who are black or Chicano or Indian or Asian or not white don't start off on an equal footing with the average middle-class white, we're looking at the act itself of the kidnapping of Patricia . . . I think this is the problem with the SLA.

Eleven weeks had now passed since the kidnapping, and two since Patty's last message. Despite his public optimism, Hearst was becoming deeply discouraged. He confided in Hiler his disappointment in the poor organisation of the PIN programme, his conviction that large amounts of food were being embezzled, and his low opinion of the FBI, who seemed no nearer locating Patty than they had been the day after the kidnapping. But Hiler urged him to try another meeting with Jefferson who had told the psychiatrist he had a new plan.

Jefferson's latest plan was that Hearst should make contact with a girl named Nancy who, said Jefferson, had continued till a month or so previously to act as a go-between carrying messages between the SLA 'combat unit' and the SLA elements inside the prison. Jefferson thought she would probably still have direct contact with the SLA in their hideout and would provide a channel whereby Hearst could negotiate directly with the kidnappers. Hearst agreed, but when Hiler drove to Nancy's Oakland address, provided by Jefferson, he found the apartment had been empty a month.

On 25 March PIN organised its biggest food distribution, the first for sixteen days. Thirty thousand people were fed in seventeen centres, and $1 million worth of food was given away.

On 28 March Hearst was told that Little and Remiro had agreed to write a letter appealing for Patty's release. There seemed no clear reason for their change of mind, but when Hearst received the letter he found it confused and ambiguous. It began by sending greetings to the SLA and curiously, to Patty, and went on to complain at length about the treatment they said they were receiving in San Quentin and to accuse the US government of a massive campaign of terrorism abroad and in the black ghettos. The letter nevertheless expressed confidence that Patty would be released unharmed. Hearst published it in the *Examiner* on 30 March.

Meanwhile, Hearst had his last meeting with Jefferson on 29 March. Cecil Williams was also present, as was Raymond Procunier. Jefferson had with him Albert Taylor and another inmate named Raymond Scott who put the view that if Patty were not released quickly, the lives of SLA sympathisers in jail would be at risk from anti-SLA inmates. He cited an article in a prison paper suggesting that if anything happened to Patty, Little and Remiro wouldn't live to stand trial. Cecil Williams quoted psychiatrist Wesley Hiler to the effect that if an acceptable formula for getting Patty out were not reached quickly, the kidnappers would soon risk their own lives in an irrational action because their psychic need for some kind of resolution was probably becoming unbearable.

Discussions returned to the formula first mooted three weeks earlier: an offer to give the kidnappers unhindered passage out of the country in exchange for Patty's release. Jefferson and Scott wanted the offer to be spelt out explicitly, but Hearst and

Williams argued that this could be counter-productive in that it would probably raise a public outcry which might force the authorities to renege on the deal.

Slowly, through the night, an agreed statement emerged. Hearst himself sat up and typed it out. On Sunday 31 March the letter appeared on the front page of the *Examiner*, signed by Clifford Jefferson, co-signed by Albert Taylor and Raymond Scott, and witnessed by Hearst and Cecil Williams.

> In furtherance to my comrades' communiqué of March 28 1974 [the Little-Remiro letter] I hereby suggest to General Field Marshal Cinque that it would be for the best interest of the poor and oppressed people to start negotiations as soon as possible with Randolph Hearst to release the prisoner of war Patricia Hearst...
>
> Negotiations should deal with any combat unit that may be pinned down in the field.

The letter proposed a meeting between the SLA, Hearst, Hallinan, Cecil Williams, Raymond Procunier and Charles Bates of the FBI to thrash out an agreement.

Next day, 1 April, Patty's sister Vicki had a letter in the *Examiner* urging the SLA to take up the offer and break their twenty-four-day silence. Randolph Hearst announced that he was putting a further $4 million into trust in San Francisco's Wells Fargo Bank, together with a legally binding agreement to release $2 million for food distribution if Patty were released unharmed by 3 May, followed, as the Corporation had promised, by a further $2 million on 2 January 1975.

The Hearsts, and the whole of America, then sat back and waited. The SLA didn't keep them waiting long.

At midday on 1 April a smartly dressed white girl walked into Crete Florists shop on Polk and Sutter Streets in downtown San Francisco and ordered $2.99 worth of red roses to be delivered to an underground newspaper called *The Phoenix*. She handed over a large white envelope and asked for it to be delivered with the flowers by 6 o'clock that evening.

The Phoenix is a small bi-weekly run by a former staffman on

Hearst's *Examiner*, John Bryan. Of the many Bay Area underground papers, it was one of the most openly sympathetic towards the SLA. An earlier edition had run what purported to be a secret, exclusive interview with SLA members but the FBI had decided it was phoney. No one could doubt the authenticity of its next scoop.

But first there was a hitch. When the florist, Mrs Kalliope Volikakis, shut up shop at the end of the afternoon and prepared to drive the roses and envelope round to *The Phoenix*, her car wouldn't start. The SLA's message spent the night behind her counter.

At 11 o'clock the next morning, seventeen hours late, *Phoenix* editor John Bryan finally took delivery. Inside the envelope was an untypically terse communiqué from 'SLA Unit 4' signed 'General Field Marshal Cin'. It stated, simply:

> Further communications regarding subject prisoner will follow in the following 72 hours. Communications will state the State, city and time of release of the prisoner.

To authenticate the message, half of Patty's driving licence, cut diagonally and including part of her photograph, was enclosed. The communiqué also included a demand that the SLA's 'Codes of War' be published by the media and a warning to Bryan that he must not co-operate with the FBI by turning over the communication.

Hearst was given the news of Patty's apparent impending release by *Examiner* city editor, Larry Drum. That night the family and Steven Weed began planning Patty's 'welcome home' party. The long nightmare, it seemed, was about to end.

Next morning, 3 April, KSAN radio received another tape. They played it over, expecting the promised details of Patty's release. Instead, they heard Patty's voice, cool and hard:

> For those who would bear the hopes and future of our people, let the voice of their guns express the words of freedom.
> I would like to begin this statement by informing the public

that I wrote what I am about to say. It's what I feel. I have never been forced to say anything on any tape. Nor have I been brainwashed, drugged, tortured, hypnotised or in any way confused. As George Jackson wrote, 'It's me, the way I want it, the way I see it.'

Mom, Dad, I would like to comment on your efforts to supposedly secure my safety. The PIN giveaway was a sham. You attempted to deceive the people. You were playing games – stalling for time – time which the FBI was using in their attempts to assassinate me and the SLA elements which guarded me. You continued to report that you did every-thing in your power to pave the way for negotiations for my release – I hate to believe that you could have been so unimaginative as to not even have considered getting Little and Remiro released on bail. While it was repeatedly stated that my conditions would at all times correspond with those of the captured soldiers, when your lawyer went to inspect the 'hole' at San Quentin, he approved the deplorable con-ditions there – another move which potentially jeopardised my safety. My mother's acceptance of the appointment to a second term as UC Regent, as you well knew, would have caused my immediate execution had the SLA been less than 'together' about their political goals. Your actions have taught me a great lesson, and in a strange kind of way, I'm grateful to you.

Steven, I know that you are beginning to realise that there it no such thing as neutrality in time of war. There can be no compromise, as your experience with the FBI must have shown you. You have been harassed by the FBI because of your supposed connections with so-called radicals, and some people have even gone so far as to suggest that I arranged my own arrest.

We both know what really came down that Monday night but you don't know what's happened since then. I have changed – grown. I've become conscious and can never go back to the life we led before. What I'm saying may seem cold to you and to my old friends, but love doesn't mean the same thing to me anymore. My love has expanded as a result of my experiences to embrace all people. It's grown into an unselfish love for my comrades here, in prison, and on the streets. A love that comes from the knowledge that 'no one is free until we are all free'. While I wish that you could be a comrade, I don't expect it – all I expect is that you try to understand the changes I've gone through.

There was a pause and a click, then Patty delivered the key sentence.

I have been given the choice of, one, being released in a safe area, or, two, joining the forces of the Symbionese Liberation Army and fighting for my freedom and the freedom of all oppressed people. I have chosen to stay and fight.

One thing which I have learned is that the corporate ruling class will do anything in their power in order to maintain their position of control over the masses, even if this means the sacrifice of one of their own. It should be obvious that people who don't even care about their own children couldn't possibly care about anyone else's children. The things which are precious to these people are their money and power – and they will never willingly surrender either. People should not have to humiliate themselves by standing in line in order to be fed, nor should they have to live in fear for their lives and the lives of their children . . .

Then followed a bitter attack on her family.

Dad, you said that you were concerned with my life and you also said that you were concerned with the life and interests of all oppressed people in this country. But you are a liar in both areas and, as a member of the ruling class, I know for sure that yours and Mom's interests are never the interests of the people. Dad, you said you would see about getting more job opportunities for the people, but why haven't you warned the people what is going to happen to them – that actually the few jobs they still have will be taken away.

You, a corporate liar, of course will say that you don't know what I am talking about, but I ask you then to prove it. Tell the poor and oppressed people of this nation what the corporate state is about to do, warn black and poor people that they are about to be murdered, down to the last man, woman, and child. If you're so interested in the people, why don't you tell them what the energy crisis really is. Tell them how it's nothing more than a manufactured strategy, a way of hiding industry's real intentions. Tell the people that the entire corporate state is, with the aid of this massive power supply, about to totally automate the entire industrial state, to the point that in the next five years all that will be needed will be a small class of button pushers; tell the people, Dad, that all of the lower class and at least half of the middle class will be unemployed in the next three years, and that the removal of expendable excess, the removal of unneeded people has already started. I want you to tell the people the truth. Tell them how the law-and-order programmes are just a means to remove so-called violent – meaning aware – individuals from the community in order to facilitate the controlled removal of unneeded labour forces from this country, in the same way that Hitler controlled the removal of the Jews from Germany.

I should have known that if you and the rest of the corporate state were willing to do this to millions of people to maintain power and to serve your needs, you would also kill me if necessary to serve those same needs. How long will it take before white people in this country understand that whatever happens to a black child happens sooner or later to a white child? How long will it be before we all understand that we must fight for our freedom?

Then, for the new Patty Hearst, a 'reborn' name.

I have been given the name Tania after a comrade who fought alongside Che in Bolivia for the people of Bolivia. I embrace the name with the determination to continue fighting with her spirit. There is no victory in half-assed attempts at revolution. I know Tania dedicated her life to the people, fighting with total dedication and intense desire to learn, which I will continue in the oppressed American people's revolution. All colours of string in the web of humanity yearn for freedom.

Osceola [Russell Little] and Bo [Joseph Remiro], even though we have never met, I feel like I know you. Timing brought me to you and I'm fighting wih your freedom and the freedom of all prisoners in mind. In the strenuous jogs that life takes, you are pillars of strength to me. If I'm feeling down, I think of you, of where you are and why you are there, and my determination grows stronger. It's good to see that your spirits are so high in spite of the terrible conditions. Even though you aren't here, you are with other strong comrades, and the three of us are learning together – I, in an environment of love, and you in one of hate, in the belly of the fascist beast. We have grown closer to the people and become stronger through our experiences. I have learned how vicious the pig really is, and our comrades are teaching me to attack with even greater viciousness, in the knowledge that the people will win. I send greetings to 'Death Row' Jeff, Al Taylor, and Raymond Scott. Your concern for my safety is matched by my concern for yours. We share a common goal as revolutionaries, knowing that Comrade George lives.

It is in the spirit of Tania that I say, 'Patria o muerte. Venceremos!' [Homeland or death. We will overcome.]

Patty's voice stopped. The tape clicked again, then continued with a message from Cinque. 'The prisoner was freed,' he said, 'but she refused to go home. There is no further need to discuss the release of the prisoner since she is now a comrade and has been accepted into the ranks of the people's army as a comrade and fighter. There is no further basis for negotiations since the subject may leave whenever she feels that she wishes to do so and she is armed and perfectly willing and able to defend herself.'

It was some hours before Randolph and Catherine Hearst, punch-drunk with disbelief, could be persuaded to make a public comment. Eventually Hearst spoke to the silent newsmen who had gathered at his door.

I think what most people would like to know is whether we believe Patty is a member of the SLA or not. Well, personally I don't believe it. We've had her for twenty years, they had her for sixty days. I don't believe she's going to change philosophies that quickly or that permanently. And I'll never believe it until she talks to me or her mother or her sisters or one of her cousins, and is freed, and free to talk without any influence on her whatsoever. At that time, if it's her choice to become a member of an organisation like this, we'll still love her and she's free to do whatever she wants, of course. After all, the FBI are not after her. She's free. The SLA could have freed her, let her come home and talk and she could have joined them at some later date. And that's just the way we feel about it.

Mrs Hearst, too upset to show herself in public, issued a written statement.

We are a close family and I cannot believe that the daughter I know so well has willingly adopted the way of life described by the SLA.

Only a few months ago, she was happily planning her wedding and a career in the field of art history. Before Christmas we went to a local store and she was terribly excited as she selected the china for her home. Patty wanted a nice wedding and was enjoying planning her honeymoon trip. Steve's plans are to be a professor and she was looking forward to a life in the academic community. She was even thinking of the possibility of attending a graduate school in the history of art.

We all spent this Christmas in the snow, and Patty, who is proud of her cooking, had brought along her file of recipes. She even treated us to some home-made cinnamon rolls.

Until the day of her capture, Patty was a young lady of great assurance, who was content with the direction in which she was going.

Only Patty, in person, can convince me that the terrible, weary words that she uttered came from her heart and were delivered by her own free will.

Steven Weed, too, was unbelieving, incapable of accepting the bitter rejection of his fiancée. He told the newsmen on Hearst's doorstep:

I'm reconciled to the idea that Patty must have, well, matured a great deal in the past two months. But it seems to me incredibly cynical on the part of the SLA to think that I can believe that Patty has refused her freedom, and even more than that, has refused to explain to me what's been on her mind the last several weeks. If she told it to me in person, I – well, I could believe it. It wouldn't be easy but I could believe it.

It just seems to me that if the SLA wants the truth to be known, they must ask Patty if she doesn't want to at least temporarily leave and speak her mind. If she only speaks it to me, that would be enough . . . I just want to tell Patty I love her as much as ever. And I think that she knows I can accept whatever she has chosen, even though it may be hard. I can accept it.

Then, without waiting to answer questions, he turned and walked back into the Hearsts' house.

What had happened in the Golden Gate Avenue apartment to turn Patty Hearst, heiress to her father's fortune, into Tania Hearst, heiress to the mantle of Che Guevara's revolutionary mistress?

Her journey had begun with a sudden, violent, brutal abduction. Her half-clothed body had been dumped, bruised and bleeding, in the boot of a car. In her terror, she must have expected a terrible death. Instead, her captors had bathed and bandaged her cuts and bruises. It must have been with a profound sense of relief that she came to realise, after the first numbing shock, that the people who had carried her off were not just common hoods on an extortion racket but young people who spoke a language of political idealism familiar to any Berkeley student. Earnest attempts were no doubt made to explain to her why it was unfortunately necessary for her to be kidnapped so that the hungry could be fed. Her father had only to dip into his pocket to secure her release. If he showed some reluctance to do so, if he started playing politics with the SLA, that showed how he really felt about his daughter. Soon she would find herself sharing her captors' anger at her father's apparent reluctance to meet the SLA's full demands, and her captors' fear of a police shoot-in. As the weeks dragged on, with little to do in an overcrowded room but read, talk, listen to music and sleep, slowly, imperceptibly, she would become one of the family, joining in their discussions, sharing their chores. And all the time the SLA, wittingly or not, would be following Jerry Rubin's advice: 'Treat her with such love and understanding that she comes away from you respecting and digging you . . . Under no circumstances harm her . . . Win her over as an ally to your cause.'

So, inevitably, the captive's political consciousness too would change and develop. Patty had never been a political animal. She had assumed the effortless liberalism of her generation, and of Berkeley in particular, but had never read a political book. Now she was given books to read and her primer, it seems, was George Jackson's *Blood in My Eye*. Jackson had sharpened the consciousness of a generation of blacks and students, and his violent death in an attempted jail-break had supercharged his eloquent words, adding another potent voice to what he himself called 'the many thunderous graveyard affirmations which for us blacks speed the revolution to its ultimate issue'.

Jackson's writings had inspired the whole spectrum of the American Left, but, in view of the SLA's hostility to the Black Panthers – in which Jackson held the honorary rank of field marshal – he is an intriguing choice as mentor and guru. DeFreeze, after all, had spent several years aiding the Los Angeles Police Department in its fight against the black Marxists of the BPP, and although his politicisation in Vacaville changed the pseudo-militancy of his LAPD-Karenga period into the genuine and recognisably Leftist militancy of the SLA, it doesn't seem to have reconciled him to the Panthers. Huey Newton, the BPP leader, was put on the SLA's death list for criticising the Foster killing. It may be that DeFreeze's hostility to Panther leaders was not, ironically, shared by his white SLA comrades. Or, more likely, it was possible to honour Jackson because he was dead, a martyr rather than a rival field marshal. Or again, it may be that the SLA honoured George Jackson because he espoused a strategy of violent revolution to which later Panther leaders merely paid lip service and which the SLA could claim only they took literally.

For George Jackson, as Patty discovered, the revolution was to be made by 'the righteous fielding of a clandestine army', a fearless band of urban guerrillas led by 'the baddest and strongest of our kind: calm, sure, self-possessed, completely familiar with the fact that the only things that stand between black men and violent death are the fast break, quick draw and snap shot'.

Jackson's vision was of America brought to its knees at home as its armies had been brought to their knees by the guerrilla fighters of Vietnam.

We must in all haste transcend the intellectual inhibitions that preclude support of at least the minimum level of violence that must develop concomitantly with each political thrust; our attitudes must change before we can expect any response from the people, workers, students, lumpen-proletariat. We must accept the eventuality of bringing the USA to its knees, accept the closing off of critical sections of the city with barbed wire, armoured pig carriers criss-crossing the city streets, soldiers everywhere, tommy-guns pointed at stomach level, smoke curling black against the daylight sky, the smell of cordite, house to house searches, doors being knocked down, the commonness of death. Then we must learn the forms of resistance: the booby trap, the silenced pistol and rifle, the pitting of streets to slow them down, the wrecking of heavy equipment to block their effi-

cient movement, false walls, hidden sub-basements, tunnels . . .
We simply stop allowing ourselves to be hunted and do some
stalking of our own . . .

Jackson laid down a blueprint for guerrilla organisation which
the SLA seems to have followed fairly closely, so far as their
natural indiscipline allowed.

Only the light, portable, easily machined or easily stolen
weapons are employed by the guerrilla under normal circumstances . . . The sniper's rifle, the light machine gun, the
silenced pistol, the flame thrower, the poison dart, poison
bullet, crossbow, the knife, the fist, all form the guerrilla
arsenal . . . All dwellings should be rented and expendable.
They should be equipped so that when forced to leave by
tunnel or other hidden exits, the place can be burned to
create further confusion for the attacker and destroy evidence.
Food and clothing should be purposely simple. Clothing must
always be available for disguises . . .

So the blacks and 'conscious whites' together would place 'a
blade in the throat of fascism. The outlaw and the lumpen will
make the revolution: the people, the workers will adopt it.'
This heroic but sadly unrealistic perspective, product of California's barbarous prison system and of a despairing reaction
against the supremacy of Nixon Man, had nowhere found a
clearer echo than among the young radicals who joined the
prison movement and saw in every black prisoner a mute,
inglorious but potentially liberated George Jackson. Nancy
Ling Perry claimed that Donald DeFreeze had 'known
courageous comrade George Jackson' in jail and that 'the
spirit of all the brothers Cinque knows lives in him now'. Perhaps Patty too, dazzled by the power of Jackson's rhetoric as
she encountered it for the first time, transferred to DeFreeze
the attributes of the dead revolutionary.
Not the least important factor in the internal dynamics of the
group was its irregular complex of sexual relationships. Donald
DeFreeze was enjoying a free sex-life more or less simul-

taneously with Nancy, Emily and Mizmoon while moving through the Berkeley underground before the kidnapping, and there is no reason to suppose these arrangements were interrupted in the Golden Gate apartment. Bill Harris was probably sleeping both with Emily and their long-time friend, Angela. Camilla and Mizmoon, though their exclusive attachment had ended a year earlier, may well have resumed their lesbian relationship. Of all the group, only Willie Wolfe was unattached.

The former pacifist whose experiences as a prison visitor turned him into a revolutionary may well have been the most attentive of Patty's captors, the one most ready with reassurance and support. She was soon to speak of the love she had found for him, describing him as 'the sweetest, gentlest man who ever lived'. Perhaps it was the combination of his gentle sensitivity and his passionate single-mindedness as a revolutionary which attracted her. Certainly now, more than ever, she must have felt the need for protective love to offset the sense of having been abandoned by her family. The girl who had had her first affair at fourteen and who later scandalised her mother by insisting on moving in with her boyfriend, once again followed her own independent, personal code. Perhaps she saw in Wolfe the quiet, teacher-like qualities that had attracted her in Steven Weed. Or, more likely, the revolutionary introduced her to adventures far beyond the scope of the quiet, staid domesticity of her relationship with Weed. Perhaps where Weed had appealed to the mother-cultivated good-little-girl side of her nature, Wolfe helped liberate the frustration and rebellion which were the hidden aspects of her adolescence. But however that may be, some time in March, within eight weeks of her violent separation from Weed, Patty's induction into the SLA's family circle was consummated by her acceptance of Wolfe as her new lover.

Having become one of the group, it seems that Patty was more or less free to come and go as she chose. The owner of the nearby New Laguna grocery store, Mrs E. Jamerson, remembers 'practically all of them' coming in at one time or another for milk, bread, frozen foods and plum wine. By the end of March or early April, says Mrs Jamerson, Patty herself was a regular customer. 'She was thin and pretty, really beautiful. Once I asked her "Are you Patty Hearst?" but she just smiled and said "A lot of folks think that".' The FBI was never quite sure how much faith to put in Mrs Jamerson's testimony, but if she had been able to put a date to Patty's first appearance – assuming the girl *was* Patty – it would have been the best available lead to the precise timing of her decision to 'stay and fight'.

As it is, the evidence remains confused, and nowhere is the confusion worse than in the timing of the two contradictory messages from the SLA, the one promising her release and the other announcing her conversion. What happened during those critical three or four days in the Golden Gate apartment?

On Thursday 28 March, Little and Remiro wrote their letter to the *Examiner*. The fact that it contained a message of greetings to Patty suggests that the San Quentin prisoners somehow knew that Patty was no longer an unwilling hostage of the SLA. The letter was published two days later on Saturday 30 March. The more important Jefferson-Taylor-Scott letter was written on the night of 29 March and published in the Sunday edition of the *Examiner* on 31 March. Next day – April Fool's day – the SLA delivered to the florist's shop the short message announcing Patty's impending release.

It was generally assumed that this last event was a direct response to the other two – that the SLA decided to respond favourably to the appeals made by its comrades in jail. But this ignores an awkward fact: the SLA message, though *delivered* after publication of the two appeals, was date-marked 29 March, before either appeal had been printed by the *Examiner*.

It could be that the SLA wrote the communiqué after reading the appeals, then pre-dated it to make it appear that the decision to release Patty had been arrived at independently rather than being forced on them by outside pressures. But this would involve a direct snub to the letter writers in prison, a message saying, in effect, 'We don't need your advice, stay out of our affairs.' The same objection arises even more strongly against the theory that the release promise was delivered on

1 April as a deliberate, cynical and cruel April Fool's joke –
a promise the SLA had no intention of keeping – for the hoax
could not be played against the Hearsts without it being an
equally brutal kick in the teeth for Little, Remiro, Jefferson,
Taylor and Scott.

The likelihood is that a counsel of moderation within the SLA
prevailed with the argument that Patty, having proved her
sympathy and goodwill, could safely be returned to the outside world. The SLA had, after all, won a colossal propaganda
victory. It had demonstrated that the rich could be forced to
feed the poor. It had extracted a promise of a $2 million down
payment, to be followed by another $2 million at the end of
the year. There was much to be gained by releasing Patty and
nothing by continuing to hold her, since her value as a hostage
was clearly reduced both by her conversion to the cause and by
Hearst's refusal or inability to deliver a higher ransom. So the
decision was taken. Patty would be released.

Was Patty perhaps not a party to the group's decision? Or
did she change her mind? She *could* go home – but did she want
to? Where was her home now? Which was her real family?
Could she go back to mother and Steven Weed, art history and
shopping for the bottom drawer? Could she leave Willie the
Wolf? Did the succession of public appeals so painstakingly
negotiated by her father have the perverse effect of hardening
her resolve never to return to a life from which she had been
liberated? As she had once announced to her mother that, like
it or not, she was going to Berkeley rather than Stanford, and as
she had once told her parents that, like it or not, she was going
to live with her boy friend, so now she told her new family,
communiqué or no communiqué, promise or no promise, she
was going to stay and fight.

When did she make the tape announcing her decision? It
couldn't have been before Sunday 31 March since her reference
to Jefferson, Scott and Taylor clearly relates to their letter
printed that morning. But the next day was the day on which,
early in the morning, the promise to release her was delivered
to the florist's. So did she make her historic recording that
Monday, knowing the release promise was already in transit?

And if not, if it was made the day before, did the SLA deliberately allow the already dishonoured promise to go on its way without recall – or did the left hand not know what the right was up to?

Whatever happened, whether the confusion was calculated or accidental, whether it reflected conflicting views within the SLA or a profound ambivalence on Patty's part, the tape which broke the news of her conversion arrived at KSAN radio the day after *The Phoenix* received the SLA's red roses and white envelope promising Patty's safe return.

Patty's wasn't the only voice on the tape. Bill Harris, introducing himself as 'Tico', castigated white radicals who were 'bold enough to intellectualise about revolution but far too chickenshit to make it'. He confessed revealingly that 'most of us have been nearly fatally stricken with the vile sickness of racism or immobilised by our sexist egos and have watched and done nothing as our sisters have rushed into battle. We have fooled ourselves into believing that Madison Avenue piggery will bring us eternal bourgeois happiness. If we haven't bought into the racist, sexist, capitalist, imperialist programme, we have "greened-out" in Mendicino and New Hampshire. To black people, who lead our struggle to freedom, we have proved to be the racist punks of the world.' But many had 'seen through this sham'. 'We know we have a long way to go to purify our minds of the many bourgeois poisons but we also know that this isn't done through bullshitting and ego-tripping . . . It is done by unleashing the most devastating revolutionary violence ever imagined.'

'Fahizah's' contribution was largely a hymn of praise to 'Cinque Mtume, Fifth Prophet', but she too had something to say about the self-purification process that would-be revolutionaries must go through: 'We must deal with all the conditions outside ourselves which oppress and enslave us, and we must deal with the enemy within.' She also spoke about death in words which only six weeks later were to assume a pathetic significance: 'He or she who is scared and seeks to run from death will find it, but she or he who is not afraid and who actively seeks death out will find it not at their door.'

'Field-Marshal' Cin's statement began with the reading of 'death warrants' against 'three agents of the enemy who have been found guilty of informing to the enemy' and should therefore be 'shot on sight by any of the people's forces'. They were Robyn Steiner, Russell Little's former girlfriend, now described as 'an informer of the FBI'; Chris Thompson, who had by now told the FBI he had sold Little the gun which police claimed had been used to kill Marcus Foster, and Colston Westbrook, the BCA co-ordinator who had first sponsored DeFreeze in Vacaville and was now described as 'an agent of the CIA, the FBI and military intelligence'.

After issuing the 'death warrants' DeFreeze closed with an incongruous, fatherly message to his children:

I would like to take this opportunity to speak to my six lovely black babies. Victor, John, Sherry, Sherlyne, Dawn and DeDe, I want you to know that to just say your names again fills my heart with joy. I want you to know that I love you with all the love that a father can have for those so dear to him. And I want you to understand also that I have not forgotten my promise to you that whenever you needed me I would be there at your side, and so I am now, even when you may not see me, I am there. Because no matter where I am, I am fighting for your freedom, your future, and your life.

Daddy wants you to understand that I can't come home because you and the people are not free, and as long as the enemy exists I can find no rest nor any hope for you or our people as a whole. I can't be happy when the enemy murders the children of other fathers and mothers. I want you to understand that I have to fight for you and for all fathers and mothers who must stay home, or who have not the courage to fight, or the clear understanding yet that the greatest gift they can give their children is freedom. So to you, my children, even when I may never see you again, know that I love you and will not for any price forsake your freedom and the freedom of all oppressed peoples.

The tape, marking the most sensational and unexpected developments yet in a story that still had its biggest climaxes to come, ended mockingly with part of a new pop release, 'Way Back Home', playfully described by DeFreeze as 'the national anthem of the Symbionese Liberation Army'. And with the tape came the crumpled polaroid photograph which was to be wired to news centres all over the world: Tania Hearst, mouth grimly set, blouse unbuttoned, legs aggressively apart, carbine at hip, posed before a huge seven-headed cobra symbol. A gun-toting Barbie-doll stalking the fascist insect which preys on the life of the people.

6 The Proof

In the nationwide orgy of speculation which followed the sensational events of the beginning of April, theory contended with theory, fact with fantasy and realism with wishful thinking. 'I know my girl very well,' said Catherine Hearst, 'and I know she would never join any organisation like that without being coerced.'

Coercion: this was the family's explanation of what had happened, and the Hearst press took it up uncritically. The *Examiner* suggested that Patty had probably made all her tape-recordings at gunpoint, reading scripts written for her by the SLA. Another theory suggested she had been brainwashed with the aid of drugs or even by more sophisticated means of sensory deprivation. The brainwashing of American prisoners captured in the Korean and Vietnam wars was cited in illustration of what 'communists' could do to the mind. The *Examiner* commissioned an analysis from a San Francisco academic described as 'an expert in the politics of revolutionary warfare and thought reform'. His conclusion was that Patty and other SLA members had been put through 'a coercive political process used to indoctrinate and condition over 750 million Chinese under the Communist dictatorship of Mao Tse-tung'.

The brainwashing theory, apart from its inherent implausibility, given what we know of the SLA's tiny scale and lack of the necessary sophistication, simply doesn't begin to hold up against the stark evidence of Patty's tapes. No objective listener to that tired, angry, embittered, betrayed voice could mistake its spontaneous authenticity for an artificially induced, zombie-like repetition of rehearsed lines and imposed responses. This theory gained ground because it was a straw to be grasped at. The Hearst family could not face the bitter truth that Patty had voluntarily rejected them and their values, so they defied the evidence and protested that Patty must have been brain-washed. And all over America a generation of identifying parents made for the same easy bolt-hole rather than face the terrifying alternative.

A further theory had it that Patty was playing the SLA along in a brilliant, desperate bid to stay alive. Surviving victims of previous kidnappings were paraded to testify that this was how they themselves had reacted. A Chicago executive kidnapped in 1973 by a non-political gang and ransomed for $1.5 million was quoted as saying: 'I would have done anything my captors wanted me to do, make a tape-recording, anything. I could do all my explaining later.' A Methodist minister's wife, kidnapped with her six-year-old daughter in November 1973, told reporters: 'Whatever they wanted, we followed their instructions. As long as you're alive, you feel you're still in the ballgame and you've got a chance of winning it.' But even if a business executive and a middle-aged Methodist had bluffed their kidnappers for the few hours they were in captivity, was it credible that nineteen-year-old Patty could do so on what would be a truly heroic scale, not for hours, days, even weeks, but months? And again, did the theory hold against the evidence of the tapes – the tell-tale tone and inflection of Patty's words?

There was revived speculation in some quarters that Patty had either been party to her own kidnapping or was already pre-disposed towards revolutionary politics by exposure to Berkeley radicalism. To the suggestion by a newsman that only a co-operative victim would bring with her the credit cards, driving licence and other personal effects so useful for the authentification of communiqués, Hearst replied hotly that kidnappers who were capable of carrying off a young girl probably wouldn't feel too inhibited about carrying off her handbag as well. And he cited the advance reference to the kidnapping found in one of the Concord documents as 'proof positive' that the kidnap plot had been real enough.

An unidentified voice on the 3 April tape had forecast that with Patty's conversion the SLA's 'pressure-point' on the media would cease and 'the fascist corporate military state, via the media' would at last feel free to vent its full fury on the SLA. Inevitably, this is just what did happen. Reporters and editors exacted revenge for their weeks of nervous compliance with SLA directives. Hearst himself, hitherto so careful to court the SLA and its friends, now spoke of them as 'nuts', 'dingbats' and 'monsters' whose demands added up to 'one of the biggest rip-offs the press has ever gone through'.

Efforts continued to be made to persuade Patty to come out and tell the world in person what she really believed. Weed made one such appeal and so did Vincent Hallinan, who had stayed on as one of Hearst's legal advisers after the secret negotiations with Jefferson. Other radical leaders continued to offer themselves as intermediaries. Dennis Banks, leader of the American Indian Movement and a hero of the 1973 occupation of Wounded Knee, appealed to the SLA to get in touch with him to arrange a meeting between Patty and her parents. There was no response.

On 7 April the Hearsts left San Francisco to spend a week with friends in Mexico. They were both tired, ill and in need of rest and privacy. The following day Steven Weed also flew south to Mexico City, but his journey had a different purpose. Weed and the Hearsts had drifted apart: only Patty had been their common bond before, and the common deprivation of her wasn't in itself strong enough to overcome the Hearsts' dislike of 'Toothbrush' and his resentment at having been effectively excluded from the family's negotiating strategy. Now Weed was striking out on his own. In Mexico City lived Régis Debray, the French Marxist writer who had championed the cause of revolution in Latin America and had been a personal friend of both Che Guevara and his mistress, the original Tania. Weed sought to enlist his help in making contact with the new Tania.

Debray agreed, somewhat reluctantly, to do what he could. He was about to leave for Paris, but drafted a letter to Patty asking her 'only to assure me that you have consciously and freely chosen to take the name and follow the example of Tania'. The letter was released in Paris on 12 April and published in the *Examiner* the same day. If Patty could be induced to reply, it would at least prove she was still alive. But the SLA had their own plans for proving that it was Tania who was very much alive.

In their Golden Gate Avenue apartment, the SLA were running out of money. Rent, food and supplies had eaten into the $1500 Camilla Hall had withdrawn in February from her Berkeley bank account. By early April Camilla was passing bad cheques on local shopkeepers. For the SLA, it was time to revive the plans carefully drawn up on paper months before but abandoned in Concord: plans for a bank robbery.

South of Golden Gate Park, only minutes from their hideout and at the centre of the appropriately named Sunset district peopled largely by the elderly and comfortably retired, the modern, plate-glass-fronted branch of the Hibernia Bank occupied the greater part of a shopping complex on Noriega Street, off 19th Avenue, the main route through the park.

During the first two weeks in April the bank was cased by the SLA, and details of its layout noted. Then on 11 April, four cars were rented from separate agencies by Angela Atwood, the Harrises and Willie Wolfe, all of whom used false names and driving licences. At least one of the cars was hired in the name and with the licence of Janet Cooper, the girl through whom Bill Harris had asked his mother to send him money two months earlier. Four days later, on Easter Monday, 15 April, the SLA again went into action.

Easter Monday is not a bank holiday in California. The Sunset branch of the Hibernian was doing business as usual. The doors were opened at nine by George Shea, the sixty-six-

year-old armed duty guard who had never had cause to use
his gun since taking up the job three years earlier. In the
middle of Golden Gate Park, two cars pulled up on 19th
Avenue and a number of empty ammunition boxes were care-
lessly tossed into a rubbish bin. The cars, a red AMC Hornet
sports and a green Ford station wagon, drove on and parked
on the unused forecourt of a petrol station closed due to the
energy crisis. The garage was right across the road from the
Hibernia Bank.

At 9.50 the station wagon swung across the road and pulled
up on the corner. Donald DeFreeze, followed by Nancy,
Mizmoon, Camilla and Patty, climbed out and ran into the
bank, each armed with a carbine. All wore blue guerrilla-style
donkey jackets and Patty wore a brown shoulder-length wig.
There was a moment of panic as Camilla, who had left her
glasses behind, stumbled at the door, dropped her carbine
magazine and scrambled frantically to retrieve the loose bullets
that spilt across the floor. But that was the only hitch. DeFreeze
was shouting. 'This is the SLA, this is the SLA! Down on the
floor or we'll blow your heads off.' Twenty bank employees
and six screaming customers did as they were told.

The bank manager, in an adjacent office, heard the screams
and looked through a window to see what was happening. De-
Freeze was disarming the guard of his revolver. The manager
knew the security cameras were on. Every move of the SLA
was being recorded on film from three angles.

DeFreeze took up position at one end of the tellers' counter
and Camilla stood guard at the other. In the centre of the lobby
stood Patty, a cartridge clip visible on the carbine which, according to witnesses who dared to look up from the floor, she carried
with confident assurance. According to bank guard Shea, she was
shouting orders and spitting out obscenities. 'Lie down or I'll
shoot your mother-fucking head off!' she screamed at the tellers
as Nancy and Mizmoon took their keys and scooped more than
$10,000 from the cash drawers. Shea and the manager, still
watching mesmerised through his peephole, told police and
reporters later they had no doubt Patty was a willing participant.
'She wasn't scared,' said Shea. 'She had a gun and looked ready

to use it. She had plenty of command in her voice and didn't falter. She meant business all right!'

Having emptied the cash drawers, the bank robbers turned to leave and as they did so, intoxicated by his triumph, the old manic trigger-happy DeFreeze of the 1960s took over for a moment from the revolutionary and he let loose a magazine of bullets through the plate-glass door, hitting two elderly passers-by, seriously wounding both in the stomach. Outside, he fired again in the direction of another onlooker, but missed. Then the five piled into the station wagon and sped away, closely followed by the Harrises, Wolfe and Angela Atwood who had all been waiting and watching in the Hornet.

Two blocks from the bank, the nine fugitives transferred to the remaining two of the four cars they had hired for the raid and made their way back to their hideout. The Hornet and the Ford station wagon were found half an hour later, the Ford with cyanide-tipped bullets scattered across the back seat. The other two cars were not picked up till nine days later when they were spotted in a car park under the Japanese Cultural Centre, long after police had virtually abandoned a city-wide search for them.

The day after the raid, the FBI released a selection of the 1200 photographs taken by the bank's cameras. They were to become the most widely syndicated pictures of their kind ever taken. All five members of the raiding party were clearly and unmistakably identifiable. Despite her wig, the girl in the centre of the lobby was undeniably Patty, as even her weary parents conceded. A warrant was issued by the FBI for her arrest as a 'material witness'. Warrants for armed robbery were issued for Nancy Ling Perry, Patricia Soltysik and Camilla Hall – but curiously not yet for DeFreeze. Further warrants followed for the Harrises, Angela Atwood and Wolfe for making false claims in obtaining false driving licences.

Across America, as yet another frontier of incredibility was breached, debate raged over whether Patty could really be a willing bank robber. The Hearsts, still insisting that Patty was being coerced, claimed that some of the bank pictures showed DeFreeze and Camilla Hall pointing their guns in Patty's direction. When George Shea gave his contrary account of Patty's language and manner, a theory was floated to the effect that the girl wasn't Patty at all but an SLA member carefully made up to look like her. But why then should she be wearing a brown wig?

One man who had no doubt that Patty was a bandit was Nixon's Attorney-General, William Saxbe, who had never found the conversion theory particularly hard to swallow since he tended to the view that most students, particularly Berkeley students, were potential subversives anyway. He described Patty bluntly as a 'common criminal' who would be treated as such. Randolph Hearst attacked the statement as irresponsible – 'the man obviously talks off the top of his head when he should be listening' – and Catherine reminded the Attorney-General that 'under American justice a person is always presumed innocent until proved guilty'. FBI Director Clarence Kelley tried to smooth things over by promising that 'the FBI will be guided by facts, not armchair opinions'. The truth was that the 160 agents assigned to the case were in no position to follow the hawks' advice to 'go in and get them': they still had no idea where the SLA and Patty were hiding.

One of the FBI's lines of inquiry involved keeping Steven Weed under secret surveillance in case Patty or her comrades made contact with him. On 21 April a young woman was arrested while talking to him in the street as they stood at the edge of a rally supporting 'Popeye' Jackson. The woman turned out to have no connection whatever with the SLA, but police explained they thought she was Emily Harris. Weed reacted angrily to the discovery that he was being followed and watched, but the fact that he was anywhere near a protest rally only added to the suspicion of those who thought he was probably a secret co-conspirator with the SLA.

There was another strange incident later the same day when the flatmate of Patty's cousin, William Randolph Hearst III, reported that he had been seized at gunpoint by three black men who released him only when he produced his driving licence to prove he wasn't a Hearst. While the incident was almost certainly not a genuine SLA operation, it had the effect of drawing a swarm of police and FBI men unwittingly closer than they had ever been before to the SLA's Golden Gate Avenue hideout, barely five minutes' walk from the young Hearst's apartment.

Meanwhile, Randolph and Catherine Hearst, abandoning hope that the FBI would ever locate the hideout, had resorted in desperation to their own pathetic means of finding Patty's whereabouts. Soon after the kidnapping Hearst had been persuaded to buy the services of a self-professed psychic who had been allowed to borrow some of Patty's clothes after promising that they would lead him to her. Hearst had fired him when within three days he ran up a hotel bill of $500 of which $300 was for drinks – all on Hearst's account. Now, two months later but no nearer knowing where Patty was hiding or being kept, he again turned to the supernatural, hiring Ed Mitchell, the prestigious former astronaut who had devoted his life since leaving the space programme to telepathy, extrasensory perception and other para-normal activities. But the man who had been to the moon was as unsuccessful as the FBI when it came to finding where on earth Patty and the SLA had their hideout.

On 23 April the FBI issued its 'wanted' poster bearing Patty's picture and adding DeFreeze's name and description to those of the girls against whom warrants had been issued earlier. The delay in naming DeFreeze, following as it did the persistent refusal of the FBI to confirm press reports that he was the man suspected of being the SLA's 'Field-Marshal Cinque', was the result of DeFreeze's old police connections. The FBI delayed going public with his name till it had fully checked out his embarrassing past in the Los Angeles Police Department. Certainly they would want to be sure, before naming him, that their quarry wasn't still on the public payroll.

Nor was the FBI alone in issuing SLA posters. Even before the bank raid, San Francisco's underground newspapers were advertising 'The World's Newest Poster – TANIA 1974 – Girl with a gun posed in front of SLA flag . . . $2.50 each, volume discounts on request.' The poster sold briskly on the Berkeley campus and appeared on walls in Oakland, Palo Alto and San Francisco's Chinatown and Mission districts. This was precisely

the development most feared by FBI investigator Charles Bates
who knew that the Bureau's best chance of catching up with
the fugitives was for them to remain isolated pariahs with no
support in the wider community. Once 'Tania' and her comrades became cult figures, counter-culture heroines and heroes,
they could seek and hope to find sanctuary if forced to break
cover.

Bates had hoped that any aura of romance the SLA might
have acquired by Patty's conversion would be quickly shattered
by DeFreeze's patent viciousness in shooting and very nearly
killing innocent passers-by on the bank raid. Indeed, some of
the agents on the case confidently let it be known that they expected a split within the SLA itself, perhaps resulting in De-
Freeze's demotion. But when the next SLA tape arrived on
the desk of San Francisco community relations director Rodney
Williams, nine days after the raid, it was still 'General Field-
Marshal Cin' who was doing the talking; and there was nothing
to suggest that his version of what had happened on the raid
had been in any way questioned by his supposedly more scrupu-
lous comrades.

I am General Field-Marshal Cin speaking. Combat operations: April 15, the Year of the Soldier. Action: appropri-
ation. Supplies liberated: one .38 Smith and Wesson revolver,
condition good. Five rounds of 158 grain .30 calibre ammo.
Cash: $10,660.02. Number of rounds fired by combat forces:
seven rounds. Number of rounds lost: five. Casualties:
people's forces, none; enemy forces, none; civilian, two.
Reason: Subject One, male. Subject was ordered to lay on
the floor face down. Subject refused order and jumped out
the front door of the bank. Therefore the subject was shot.
Subject Two, male. Subject failed or did not hear warning to
clear the street. Subject was running down the street towards
the bank and combat forces accordingly assumed subject
was an armed enemy forces element. Therefore the subject
was shot.

We again warn the public: any citizen attempting to aid,
to inform or assist the enemy of the people in any manner

will be shot without hesitation. There is no middle ground in war. Either you are the people or the enemy. You must make the choice.

But once again the drama of DeFreeze's words was totally eclipsed by that of a further message from Patty on the same tape. For the first time, Patty addressed herself not to her parents but to 'the people'. Her message was chillingly clear: she had freely participated in the bank raid as 'a soldier in the people's army'. With unprecedented bitterness she derided her family as pigs and her 'ex-fiancé' as a clown.

Greetings to the people, this is Tania. On April 15 my comrades and I expropriated $10,660.02 from the Sunset Branch of Hibernia Bank. Casualties could have been avoided had the persons involved kept out of the way and co-operated with the people's forces until after our departure.

I was positioned so that I could hold customers and bank personnel who were on the floor. My gun was loaded and at no time did any of my comrades intentionally point their guns at me. Careful examination of the photographs which were published clearly shows this was true.

Our action of April 15 forced the corporate state to help finance the revolution. In the case of expropriation, the difference between a criminal act and a revolutionary act is shown by what the money is used for.

Unlike the money involved in my parents bad faith gesture to aid the people, these funds *are* being used to aid the people, and to insure the survival of the people's forces in their struggle with and for the people.

To the clowns who want a personal interview with me – Vincent Hallinan, Steven Weed and Pig Hearst – I prefer giving it to the people in the bank. It's absurd to think that I could surface to say what I am saying now and be allowed to freely return to my comrades. The enemy still wants me dead. I am obviously alive and well.

As for being brainwashed, the idea is ridiculous to the point of being beyond belief. It's interesting the way early reports characterised me as a beautiful, intelligent liberal, while in more recent reports I'm a comely girl who's been brainwashed. The contradictions are obvious.

Consciousness is terrifying to the ruling class and they will do anything to discredit people who have realised that the only alternative to freedom is death and that the only way we can free ourselves of this fascist dictatorship is by fighting, not with words but with guns.

As for my ex-fiancé, I'm amazed that he thinks that the first thing I would want to do, once freed, would be to rush and see him. I don't care if I ever see him again. During the last few months Steven has shown himself to be a sexist, ageist pig [ageist: one who discriminates on the basis of age].

Not that this is a sudden change from the way he always was. It merely became blatant during the period when I was still a hostage. Frankly Steven is the one who sounds brainwashed. I can't believe that those weird words he uttered were from his heart. They were a mixture of FBI rhetoric and Randy's simplicity.

I have no proof that Mr Debray's letter is authentic. The date and location he gave were confusing in terms of when the letter was published in the papers. How could it have been written in Paris and published in your newspapers on the same day, Adolf? In any case, I hope that the last action has put his mind at ease. If it didn't, further actions will.

To those people who still believe that I am brainwashed or dead, I see no reason to further defend my position. I am a soldier in the people's army. Patria o muerte. Venceremos.

To millions across America the venomous tone in which Patty spoke her message at last clinched the argument over whether her conversion was real or phoney, voluntary or coerced. But there still remained many who could not accept so bleak and terrifying a scenario. Among them, inevitably, were the Hearsts. 'The only good thing is that she is alive,' commented Randolph. 'Regarding her personal attacks on me, if she has been brainwashed, and I firmly believe she has, then it's not surprising she would say something like this. No matter what she says we still love her.'

Thirteen weeks had now passed since the kidnapping. In that time the SLA had forced a $2 million food distribution programme, commandeered pages of newspaper space and hours of broadcasting time, sprung a convert from the heart of the enemy camp and carried out the most publicised cash raid since Britain's great train robbery. Their operations were carried out under the noses of nearly two hundred FBI agents assigned to the case, who, with the local police, still had not the faintest idea where the group was hiding out. There seemed no reason why the SLA should not continue to lie low and run rings round the impotent law enforcement agencies.

But towards the end of April a number of factors combined to persuade the SLA to move from their Golden Gate Avenue hideout. For a start, they were no longer an anonymous group: the bank robbery, while proving Patty's allegiance to them, had also revealed their own identities, and their pictures were in every newspaper and on every television news programme. Their neighbours might recognise them. So too might the local shopkeepers. Wigs and theatrical make-up had seen them through so far, but there was a limit to the protection afforded by amateur disguises.

Then, as a Federal grand jury began its public hearings into the bank robbery, former acquaintances of SLA members were called to tell what they knew about the organisation. Janet Cooper, whose driving licence had been used to hire at least one of the bank raid get-away cars, said she had never belonged to the SLA and knew nothing. A girl named Mary Alice Siem came forward to claim that she and Thero Wheeler had quit the group before the kidnapping. Cynthia Garvey and Paul Halverson, former friends of Camilla Hall, declined to say anything at all, and for their refusal were sent to jail. But the strain on the SLA, knowing that their former friends and associates were now under pressure to talk, must have been considerable, the more so if any one of those summoned by the grand jury knew –

as at least two almost certainly did – where the hideout was.

The third factor prompting a move was the 'Zebra' manhunt. In an effort to gather information on the dozen arbitrary and still unsolved race murders which held San Francisco whites in a grip of terror, Mayor Alioto had authorised the police to stop and question any black on the city streets – a move which caused intense resentment in the black communities. It was widely expected that this would be followed by house-to-house searches in black and mixed areas. DeFreeze spoke of the likelihood of such a move in the post-robbery tape, and Willie Wolfe added a postscript accusing 'the pigs and the fascist media' of linking the 'Zebra' killings to the SLA by issuing an identikit drawing of the killer 'which has a resemblance to General Field-Marshal Cinque'. The SLA's fears that they might be caught in a net cast for other fish must have proved a powerful impetus to get out of the city while there was still reasonable freedom of movement. On 23 April they were encouraged in this view by a letter from the Black Liberation Army, received at KQED television, urging the SLA to move their operations out of the Bay Area and to spread them to the rest of the country before the 'Zebra' manhunt blocked all escape routes.

Precisely how and when they moved is still uncertain. What is known is that on 1 May a black woman giving the name 'M. Jackson' paid $375 cash to rent an apartment in the industrial and largely black Bayview district of San Francisco, barely a block away from one of the PIN distribution sites. Neighbours later reported that three black men in army-style jackets also used the apartment.

It now seems likely that this new sanctuary was rented not by the SLA themselves but by supporters, perhaps members of the Black Liberation Army. The intention was probably not to make a new SLA headquarters but to provide a stepping-stone from which the SLA could make good its escape south. Evidence found there when police raided the apartment three weeks later suggested that DeFreeze and perhaps four others had moved in from Golden Gate Avenue and that at least some of the party had stayed till the morning of 16 May – the last day for which a newspaper was found. Another SLA party may have gone straight from Golden Gate Avenue to Los Angeles: an 'advance guard' as the SLA were later to describe it.

However DeFreeze divided his troops, what is clear is that the SLA had quit 1827 Golden Gate Avenue by 1 May. Before leaving, they painted slogans and crude cobra symbols all over the walls. 'Freedom is the will of life!' was spray-painted behind the bed, and signed 'Cinque'. Others were signed 'Tania'.

Garbage was left strewn about the kitchen and on 2 May a neighbour spotted an army of cockroaches crawling out under the door. He called sanitary officials who, finding the door secured by no less than six locks, called the police. Breaking into the apartment, policemen and FBI agents were left in no doubt that they had at last stumbled on the SLA's long-sought hideout. Documents and the key to one of the bank robbery getaway cars lay in the bath, which was half-filled with an acid solution: another of Nancy Ling Perry's bizarre and botched attempts to destroy evidence. Over the bath was written a 'Warning!' to the FBI: 'Remember that you are not bullet-proof'. In the other rooms were found assorted gun parts and a lunchbag full of carbine and rifle cartridges from which the powder had been removed, leading police to speculate that the SLA had been building a home-made bomb. Wigs, clothing, a bicycle and DeFreeze's own trade mark, a stack of empty plum wine bottles, completed the haul. But Patty and the SLA had been gone twenty-four hours or more. And when they made their next public appearance it was 400 miles south, in De-Freeze's old stamping ground: Los Angeles.

7 Counter-Revolution

ACCORDING to San Francisco police records, the owner of a
certain red and white Volkswagen van bought from a second-
hand car dealer around the end of April was a Ricky Delgato
of 710 Fillmore Street. But the police never found Mr Delgato.
When they called at his address late on the evening of 16 May,
they found themselves facing not a house or an apartment block
but a vacant lot, unoccupied for twenty years. Once again the
SLA had got away with the use of false credentials to obtain a
get-away vehicle.

Some time early in May the van left San Francisco for Los
Angeles. Inside were Bill and Emily Harris and Patty Hearst.
Maybe together with them, maybe on separate trips, the rest of
the SLA travelled in two more cars bought with the proceeds of
the Hibernia bank raid: a Bonny and Clyde convoy of nine
revolutionaries complete with parcels of shotguns and cyanide-
tipped bullets, crudely painted cobra emblems and bundles of
leaflets promising death to the fascist insect.

There are three routes from the Bay Area to Los Angeles.
State Highway One, freeway all the way, is the fastest: even
with the fuel-crisis speed limit of 50 mph, the 400 miles could
be covered in just over eight hours. But the road is a happy
hunting ground for highway patrols and drivers are subject to
random spot checks. The SLA probably chose not to go that
way.

The quieter of the two alternatives is the old Spanish Missionary road up the Pacific coast, Route 101. On the right, for the driver travelling south, is an apparently endless succession of beaches and rocky headlands. On the left lie the forests of Big Sur and the wilderness of the Californian mountains. With its inconspicuous pull-ins and easy access to a maze of mountain tracks, Route 101 is custom-built for runaways. The SLA surely came this way.

They would have passed Monterey and Carmel with their prim private houses: a monied world which was all Patty had known until barely three months earlier. A little south, Patty would recognise that the range of tumbled hills on the left had once been part of the vast coastal ranch owned by her legendary grandfather, extending a full fifty miles along the Pacific. And high above San Simeon village she and her companions could have made out the twin towers of Citizen Kane's Xanadu: Hearst Castle. Patty had last been there four months earlier after the Christmas announcement of her engagement to Steve. They had surveyed the art treasures which still belonged to the family and picked those they thought they might wheedle out of her father for their new home. What thought of all this did Tania have now as the van sped past the gates and on to Los Angeles?

While San Francisco is compact and well-defined, Los Angeles is a shapeless sprawl of formerly independent cities where a journey 'across town' can mean a trip of fifty miles. The only SLA member to whom Los Angeles was familiar ground was DeFreeze and it is doubtful whether even he had much knowledge of the area outside the black ghettos of Watts and Compton, which were clearly not the best hiding places for a predominantly white guerrilla band. So the new arrivals began their house-hunting in an area skirting the campus of Pepperdine University, where they could hope to hide themselves in the transience of familiar student rooming land.

On Thursday 9 May a junior high-school teacher named Valma Davies took a call about a one-bedroom, unfurnished apartment she was advertising in the *Los Angeles Sentinel*. The woman caller persuaded Mrs Davies to drop the rent from $75 to $70 a month. That afternoon, Patty, the Harrises and possibly others moved into the tiny apartment at 833 West 84th Street.

For a week, it seems, they lived there quietly, stocking up with canned foods which they piled up on the kitchen floor. There was no furniture and they lived out of suitcases. Neighbours who noticed their comings and goings wondered why the two girls wore huge, unnatural wigs, one black, one auburn. But if the disguises were theatrical they were also effective. No one recognised the face of the best-known fugitive in America, despite the encouragement of a well publicised $50,000 reward offered by Hearst on 3 May for information leading to Patty's release. It was exactly a week after moving in that they began the string of mistakes which brought their revolution to an abrupt and terrible end.

The first mistake was trivial in kind but catastrophic in effect. On the morning of Thursday 16 May, one of the party parked the red and white Volkswagen van right outside the house. That day parking happened to be prohibited for street cleaning. The van was booked and a citation was filled out and left in the glove compartment. The citation included the 833 West 84th Street address.

Patty and the Harrises evidently didn't intend to stay long on West 84th Street. They had conceived a new plan. As the original Tania had fled with Che to the sanctuary of the hills, so the SLA prepared to make its base in the Californian wilderness. America's urban guerrilla army had decided to go rural.

They had first to re-equip themselves with protective clothing against the cold of the mountains and to buy new gear. So, a few hours after the police had booked them for their parking offence, Patty and the Harrises drove to a camping and outdoor pursuits shop, Mel's Sporting Goods, in Greenshaw Boulevard, Inglewood. Patty stayed outside in the van while Bill and Emily went inside and spent $31.50 on heavy outdoor clothing. As they were about to leave, the shop assistant saw Bill push up his sleeve what he at first thought was a pair of heavy-duty socks but later turned out to be an ammunition bandolier. The assistant, a tough twenty-year-old named Tony Shepard who was used to handling shop-lifters, followed the couple out and demanded to see what Harris had up his sleeve. Harris panicked and tried to make a break for the waiting van. The store manager came running out and there was a scuffle, during which a revolver clattered to the ground from Harris's waistband. Shepard managed to clamp a pair of handcuffs on Harris when suddenly a burst of automatic gunfire sent bystanders running for cover. From the van, Patty had let loose thirty shots, aiming over the heads of the struggling group in the doorway and spraying the wall above. In the confusion, Bill and Emily broke free and jumped into the van, which sped away. Shepard leapt into his own car and tried to follow, but lost them.

Four blocks down the road the van turned right into Ruthelen Street, then came to a halt. The first car to pull up behind was a Pontiac. As it stopped, Bill and Emily ran over and hijacked it, Emily with a small automatic which she kept pointed to the ground and Bill with a large calibre automatic which he pointed at the terrified driver and his woman passenger. 'We are the SLA and we need your car,' said Bill. 'Get out – I don't want to kill you.'

The couple got out and ran into a nearby house. There they watched Patty pass out weapons from the van to the Pontiac, which was then driven away. But Patty left two items behind in the van. A twenty-five-loop shotgun belt was left on the back seat; and crucially, the seemingly trivial parking ticket, filled out with the West 84th Street address, was left in the glove compartment.

Police found them when they were called to the van minutes later. But even when the terrified couple who had been turned out of their Pontiac told them the hijackers had announced themselves as the SLA, the police failed to appreciate what they were on to. After all, every fashionable petty crook was taking the SLA's name in vain and there was so far no good reason to believe the real SLA had ever left San Francisco. So it was another thirteen hours before the address on the parking ticket was checked out, and even longer before the gun Bill Harris had dropped outside Mel's Sporting Goods was traced as the revolver bought by Emily Harris in October 1973.

To the fleeing trio, however, it must have seemed that discovery was imminent – especially when their hijacked Pontiac stalled within minutes and refused to respond to their frantic efforts to get it going again. A father and son standing in a nearby driveway came to offer help; Bill Harris pointed a sub-machine gun at them and commandeered their Chevrolet Nova, again in the name of the SLA. It was 4.40 pm, less than ten minutes since the Harrises had walked out of the Inglewood shop, and already they were on their third get-away car.

The Chevrolet was driven across Western Avenue and the Harlow Freeway into the comparative if temporary sanctuary of the Watts ghetto. But the trio must have realised that within a very short time police all over the city would be looking for the stolen car. They must also have remembered with something close to panic the tell-tale parking ticket in their abandoned van, which meant that their 'safe house' must surely be rumbled within a matter of hours, if the police were not already on the doorstep.

Patty and Emily had two priorities. One was to get Bill Harris out of the handcuffs snapped on his wrists by Shepard. The other must surely have been to warn their comrades that the SLA's presence in Los Angeles was now known to the police and that 833 West 84th Street was no longer a safe rendezvous. To get the handcuffs off they needed to find somewhere they could buy a hacksaw: to warn their friends they needed to locate them. Both meant travelling, which they could not safely do in a stolen car. They had to find a vehicle which wasn't being sought by, and wouldn't attract the attention of, the police. As luck would have it, a suitable vehicle presented itself.

Eighteen-year-old high-school student Tom Matthews was watching television in his parent's home at 10871 Elm Street, Lynwood, two or three miles east of Watts, when just before seven o'clock there was a knock on the front door. A woman whom he later identified as Emily Harris pointed to the dark blue Ford van parked at the kerbside with a 'For Sale' sign in the windscreen, and asked if it was his. He said it was. She asked if she could have an immediate test drive. Matthews grabbed the keys and went outside with her. She was alone.

When she had driven a hundred yards or so, she suddenly pulled up beside a couple standing at the roadside. The woman was wearing a dark Afro-style wig, sweater, slacks and a new pair of hiking boots. The man carried something in a blanket, which also hid his hands. They climbed into the van and the man spoke to Matthews. 'We're the SLA. Do what you're told and you'll be OK.' The astonished boy, more intrigued than frightened, was told to get into the back of the van. He watched in amazement as Harris unwrapped two automatic rifles and two pistols and told him to cover himself with the blanket. Before he did so he noticed the handcuffs on Harris's hands.

Harris took the passenger's seat and Patty climbed into the back with Matthews. 'This is Tania,' said Harris in a matter-of-fact tone. 'You probably know who she is.' Matthews mumbled that he wasn't sure, and he was telling the truth. In the whole Los Angeles area it would probably have been impossible to find anyone less impressed by the SLA's mystique. Tom Matthews only read the baseball pages of the newspapers, and his biggest worry as the evening wore on was that his captors might make him miss the next day's match in which he was playing first base for Lynwood against Bassett.

Lying under the blanket, Matthews listened to what he could hear of the half-whispered conversation and gathered that his kidnappers were going in search of a hacksaw. The van stopped and Emily got out, returning shortly with a shopping-bag containing a new saw and a packet of blades. The van then moved on to a drive-in cinema at Inglewood which was showing a cops-and-robbers feature, *The New Centurions*. In the darkness, surrounded by other cars where the occupants were absorbed either in celluloid shoot-outs or more private back-seat pursuits, Patty and Emily took it in turns to hack their way through Bill's handcuffs. It was nearly midnight before they were through. Then they drove off, he wasn't sure where. Away from the reflected light of the cinema screen, Tom Matthews was at last allowed to come out from under his blanket. He suggested tentatively that he would like to go home now. Addressing him for the first time, Patty said she was sorry but he couldn't do that just yet.

As Emily drove across Los Angeles, Tom and Patty drifted into conversation. Tom asked what it was all about: were they really the SLA? Yes, said Patty, they really were, and they had come to start a revolution in Los Angeles. Lots of people were joining. Would Tom like to join? Tom said he'd have to think about it. Patty showed him how to load an automatic rifle.

The van made two stops and Patty told Tom she was sorry but he would have to go under the blanket again because they didn't want him to see where they were. Again it was Emily who left the van and there seems little doubt that the purpose of her two calls was to see, or leave messages for, the main body of the SLA. After the second call, Matthews gathered that the man Emily wanted to see wasn't at home.

The aimless journey continued and young Matthews again emerged from his blanket to ask Patty the questions every Pulitzer-prize-seeking reporter in America would have given his right arm to put to her. Why had she joined the SLA? Because her family weren't interested in her and her father had spent 'only' $2 million on 'garbage'. Had she joined of her own free will or was she forced to? Patty pulled a face. 'Do I look brainwashed to you?' Then she went on to tell him in detail how the Hibernia bank raid was planned and what her role was. She and her comrades had left San Francisco 'a few days back' because 'the pigs were closing in on us'. She ended by explaining why they were now on the run, proudly describing her own role in rescuing Bill and Emily from the 'pig agents' who had tried to arrest them at Mel's Sporting Goods shop that afternoon.

Then Tom said he was sorry but he really *had* to get home; it was half-way through the night and his parents would be frantic. By now they would have reported him and the van missing. He was told he would have to wait until they had found another car. So he pulled the blanket over himself and dropped off to sleep. When he awoke the van was in the Hollywood hills and it was nearly dawn. He heard the trio discussing how to hijack another car.

Frank Sutter was driving home after an all-night party when he saw two girls hitch-hiking in the early morning light. It was

6.30. He stopped, obligingly, to find Emily pointing a gun at him. She took over the wheel, and Sutter was ordered into the back seat with Patty. Emily drove to where Tom Matthews' van was parked a short distance away. Bill Harris transferred the guns to Sutter's car, told Matthews to lie face down and stay still for ten minutes and got in beside Emily. Matthews did as he was told, having first been reminded that the SLA knew where he lived and would be calling again if he raised the alarm. Frank Sutter's car sped away, and the one exclusive 'interview' given by Tania was at an end.

Matthews dutifully waited ten minutes, then drove home to tell his parents and waiting policemen he was sorry to be out so late but the SLA had kidnapped him. The incredulous police took down his statement, but he didn't mention Patty or his conversations with her. Only when Patty's fingerprints were found in the car did he tell the full story, giving so detailed an account of Patty's version of the bank robbery that the FBI couldn't doubt he was telling the truth.

Meanwhile, a somewhat tired Tom Matthews managed to make the baseball game on that Friday afternoon. To the reporters and photographers who clustered around him he would only say he felt great, thank you, and nothing much had happened, really. And the day ended well. Lynwood had an easy win over Bassett.

The Los Angeles Police Department has a round-the-clock job logging the city's reported robberies, shooting, muggings and car thefts. The report that came through at 4.35 pm on 16 May of what seemed to be the armed robbery of a pair of socks may have sounded a shade bizarre, but it wasn't treated as being exceptionally sinister. And even when it was followed by reports that two cars had been hijacked in the same area by a trio claiming to be SLA, the crime desk didn't become unduly excited. Only when the Inglewood robbers' red and white Volkswagen was found to have a San Francisco registration did the police become interested, and their suspicions were heightened when, late that evening, they heard from San Francisco that the car was registered in the name of Ricky Delgato, who turned out not to exist.

At the same time, Los Angeles received the result of a check on the gun dropped outside Mel's Sporting Goods and learned it was registered in the name of Emily Harris. The acting director of the Los Angeles FBI office, William A. Sullivan, was called in and he spotted what the city police had missed: the parking ticket carrying the 833 West 84th Street address.

Just after 6 am – when, in the nearby hills, Patty and the Harrises were preparing to abandon Tom Matthews and hijack their fourth car – a massive force of eighty police and FBI agents, armed with shotguns, rifles and tear gas, cordoned off a four-block area around the house. Snipers took up positions on surrounding rooftops and watched for signs of movement inside.

At 9 am, after what the waiting police interpreted as a sinister silence, canisters of tear gas were lobbed through the windows. Minutes later, the house was charged and broken into by fifteen flak-jacketed men from the Los Angeles Police Department's Special Weapons and Tactics unit, the anything-goes subversion-busting 'SWAT' squad. They found it empty. But in a suitcase were two credit cards, one belonging to Patty Hearst and the other to Steven Weed. There could no longer be any doubt: the SLA was in town.

As police carried out suitcases, wigs, cartons of food and reams of leaflets, agents questioned the neighbours. From them they got descriptions of two more vans which had been parked outside the house the previous day, vans they suspected belonged to the rest of the group. Within two hours, by mid-morning on 17 May, the vans had been found less than four miles away in the Compton district.

At about the same time, Patty and the Harrises relieved Frank Sutter of $250 from his wallet, telling him to 'figure this as a loan, but you won't get it back', then dropped him in the middle of Griffith Park, Hollywood. Helpless, he watched them drive off in his car.

*

At four o'clock on the morning of Friday 17 May, while Patty, the Harrises and kidnapped Tom Matthews were still driving around the Hollywood hills, and just two hours before police first staked out the house at 833 West 84th Street, the two vans seen earlier by neighbours drew up outside a tiny chalet-bungalow in the all-black district of Compton, south-central Los Angeles.

Despite the lateness of the hour, the lights were still on at 1466 East 54th Street. Inside lived two women, Christine Johnson and Emily Lewis, and Emily's five children. That night there were others in residence: a seventeen-year-old girl named Brenda Daniels and three young men: James Johnson (no relation of Christine, though reporters later took him to be a son), Clarence Ross and Freddie Freeman. Visitors were common at 1466. It was the local red-light crash-pad.

The visitor who stepped out of one of the vans and knocked on the door at 4 am was Donald DeFreeze. The SLA's field marshal said he and his friends were stranded and needed somewhere to stay. Could the sisters help? He held out $100 in notes and the women said yes, they would help. DeFreeze said that, by the way, his friends were white. He was told they would be welcome: there was no colour bar at 1466.

A white man and four girls began unloading 'luggage' from the vans. It took them a full twenty minutes to carry in a succession of heavy wooden crates. All five whites – Willie Wolfe, Nancy, Angela, Mizmoon and Camilla – wore dark green turtle-necked sweaters, blue trousers and heavy boots – a commando-style uniform. Camilla may have brought her pet Persian kitten. None of them made any effort to conceal the pistol holsters in their belts or the knives sewn into their trousers. DeFreeze paid James Johnson $30 in notes to pack the crates away in the storage 'crawl-space' under the chalet floor boards. Someone else drove the vans round the block into 53rd Street and parked them on waste ground just behind the house.

Why did the SLA party surface in so preposterously conspicuous a manner? It seems they had been in Los Angeles for at least a day or two – long enough for their vehicles to have been spotted by neighbours at West 84th Street. Somehow, either from radio news bulletins or because the Harrises had managed to call on them during their night drive, they learnt of the shoot-out at the Inglewood sports shop and decided on flight. DeFreeze may have known of the 'open house' on East 54th Street, Compton, in the heart of what must once have been familiar territory. Alternatively, the party may have headed into what they assumed to be the safety of a black ghetto and knocked up the only house still showing a light. No doubt they had an unquestioning faith in their own propaganda: they were a people's army, the vanguard of the oppressed, and the admiring blacks of the ghetto would give them sanctuary.

A more interesting but dubious theory explored by newsmen but discarded by the police had it that the SLA party were expected at East 54th Street, which they intended to make their Los Angeles base. According to young James Johnson, who was later to give an odd interview to *Newsweek* magazine, Christine Johnson had met DeFreeze on a trip to San Francisco and had offered her home as a temporary base. But James Johnson was an unreliable witness: he assured other newsmen that Patty had been among DeFreeze's party in the Compton House, which must clearly have been either invention or mistaken identity. The probability remains that DeFreeze's four o'clock knock on the door was what Christine Johnson and Emily Lewis later claimed it to be: an unplanned, unexpected and unwanted arrival.

Once inside with their 'luggage', it seems the newcomers characteristically made no secret of who they were. DeFreeze introduced himself as Cinque and his comrades as members of the SLA. They had come to Los Angeles he said, to fight for the rights of the needy and to start a revolution. The 'pigs' were after them, but the SLA would fight to the death and take as many 'pigs' with them as they could. It was familiar black ghetto rhetoric and the SLA's hosts would have heard it all before. They claimed later that they didn't take it seriously and never thought to link their guests with Patty Hearst's kidnapping.

No one got much sleep. At dawn, Brenda Daniels awoke and was introduced to the new guests. Nancy, Mizmoon, Angela and Camilla whispered together in a corner. Willie Wolfe sat on a top bunk bed, twirling his pistol, cowboy-style. DeFreeze explained to the bewildered girl that they were the SLA, then gave her $30 and asked her to go and buy some food. James Johnson was sent out for beer and plum wine. They both returned without calling the police. Both said later that the SLA had threatened to kill someone in the house if they didn't come back.

As the morning wore on, a succession of visitors called at the house, drank a can of beer with the SLA's compliments, and were allowed to leave. One was eighteen-year-old Stephanie Reed, who lived just across the street. She found Nancy and Camilla cutting sandwiches while Mizmoon and Angela packed guns and ammunition into backpacks. She asked what they were doing and one of the girls told her: 'We're gonna start a revolution and we need some black people to help us. How about you?' Stephanie said she'd think about it and left hurriedly.

DeFreeze sat out on the front porch, playing with his commando knife and chatting to one of the overnight visitors, a black man named Freddie Freeman. It is possible DeFreeze knew Freddie from his earlier life in Los Angeles. Freddie too had a record of gun offences, parole violations and associating with known felons. He may also have been a petty informer for the police. DeFreeze told him the vehicles the SLA had arrived in were no longer 'safe', and gave him $500 to go and buy a second-hand station-wagon. Freeman left the house and never returned. He had no intention of buying a vehicle for DeFreeze, and after an unsuccessful attempt to 'borrow' his employer's car, made off with the $500. The SLA had been conned. Police caught up with him later and turned him into a star witness against the SLA.

While DeFreeze and his friends waited, Emily Lewis's children arrived home from school, having left the house that morning unaware that half a dozen of the country's most wanted fugitives were in the back bedroom. They arrived home to find it apparently occupied by armed whites and alarmed and frightened, ran out into the street. DeFreeze called them from the porch, but eleven-year-old Timmy, the eldest, ran off to find his grandmother, Mrs Mary Carr, who lived in the next block. Mrs Carr called to see for herself, spotted the white girls and their guns and then did what none of the other visitors had done. She called the police.

By now, children were dashing up and down the street with the exciting news that 'those SLA people' were right there on their own block. There were more curious visitors. Two more women who came and went reported to the police. DeFreeze asked his hosts whether there was any sign of 'pigs'. He was told they were 'all over the place – probably busting folk for grass'. He seemed reassured. At 4 pm Brenda Daniels was sent out on another shopping trip. This time a patrol intercepted her on her way back.

The police had in fact been no more than a block away since mid-morning. An alert had gone out for the two SLA vans after their registration numbers had been picked up in the dawn raid at West 84th Street, and at 10 am two patrolmen spotted them in 53rd Street. They sounded the alarm.

Police and FBI called a planning meeting for 2 pm at Los Angeles Police Department headquarters in Newton Street. Assistant Police Chief Daryl Gates argued out with the FBI's local director, William Sullivan, the question of which force should lead the operation against the SLA. The issue was never in real doubt. The LAPD is the toughest police department in the West and its Special Weapons and Tactics squad (SWAT), equipped as a para-military rather than a civil police unit, was already standing by. Sullivan agreed to play the inevitable second fiddle. Captain Marvin King, head of the LAPD Investigative Headquarters Bureau, was given charge of the operation. His first move was to call in the department's public relations chief, Peter Hagan, telling him: 'What's coming down now will need a helluva lot of smart PR.'

A command post was established in an unmarked police van parked on the corner of 57th Street and Compton Avenue. It got off to a bad start. The adjacent building where officers planned to make and receive telephone calls was locked and no one had thought to bring the key. At 3 pm the command post was moved to a parking lot on Alameda Street, nearly three-quarters of a mile from the 54th Street address and the SLA vans. The car park attendant let the police use the office phones and a comprehensive short-wave radio system was also installed. By 3.30, 150 Los Angeles policemen, 100 FBI agents, 100 sherrif's officers and fifteen State Highway Patrolmen were assigned to what had now become one of the biggest operations in the LAPD's long, ruthless history.

Among the first to arrive at the command post were a squad of nineteen SWAT men. They put on bullet-proof vests and fireproof overalls and retired to a corner of the parking lot for an informal briefing. No one, they were told, was to take chances. The SLA were killers and SWAT was going to get them. Then the squad was told two stories to stoke up their righteous anger: one, that the SLA had been responsible for the murder of a policeman in the area two weeks earlier (which wasn't true), and the other, that the terrorist band was headed by a former LAPD agent who had turned traitor. So the SWAT squad collected their semi-automatics and prepared to do their duty.

By 5 pm the parking lot was full not only of the assorted faces of law and order but also of an army of newspaper reporters and photographers and television and radio crews. The word had spread that the long run of the SLA was nearly over. One question above all others dominated the thoughts of police and newsmen: was Patty with them?

Inside the command post there was continuing confusion. First target of the operation had been the plot of ground on 53rd Street where the SLA vans had been spotted that morning. Nearby was a semi-derelict house with boarded-up windows, and it was assumed that this could be the SLA's hideout. Then had come Mrs Carr's report, switching attention to 54th Street. When the huge array of police and reporters moved off from the command post just after 5 pm, half of them surrounded the empty house in 53rd Street while the rest moved on to 54th. The LAPD and its SWAT squad were taking no chances.

Within minutes it was apparent that the 53rd Street house was empty. While armed police were gingerly encircling it, a young woman TV reporter impatiently walked up to the building and knocked on the front door. When there was no answer she retreated and three flak-jacketed policemen walked up to the house, peered into the building through the spaces between the window boards, and retreated in turn. There was a brief consultation, then police and reporters moved on together to 54th Street.

Here too there was confusion. Astonishingly, the SWAT squad at first surrounded the wrong house and stood with their backs to the SLA until a small boy playing on the street pointed out where the 'whites' were staying. Having finally located the right house and redeployed accordingly, a warning was delivered at 5.44 pm by loud-hailer: 'This is the police. We want you to come right on out with your hands in the air. The house is surrounded.'

There was silence. A crowd had now gathered and only a half-hearted effort was made to disperse it.

Inside the house, the mixed group of nonchalant freedom-fighters and half-drunk visitors must suddenly have become aware of their danger. Christine Johnson started screaming and was beaten into silence by two of the SLA girls. Eight-year-old Tony Lewis was picked up by one of the girls and popped into the bath-tub where he was told to stay and keep his head down. Clarence Ross, who remembered little else of what happened that afternoon, ran from the house and was lucky not to have been shot dead on the doorstep. He was quickly bundled into a police van and driven away.

Five minutes later the police broadcast a second loud-hailer warning. This time Tony Lewis ran out of the house. He was apparently allowed to leave as the SLA made their fateful decision to stay and fight it out. Police Captain Marvin King decided to smoke out the fugitives with CS gas, and just before 6 pm the first two canisters of police-issue Flite-rite were fired through the windows.

There was no response. The fugitives evidently had gas masks. King ordered a fusilade of gas in an attempt to overload the masks. This time there was an answering rifle shot from the house, and battle was joined.

Police and FBI men returned fire simultaneously from four armour-protected entrenchments. Then there was a burst of

machine-gun fire from the house which stitched an erratic per-
foration into parked cars and houses opposite. Realising for the
first time the strength of fire-power the SLA had at its disposal,
King ordered up four machine-guns from his Metropolitan
Division. He also radioed police headquarters for permission to
use fragmentation grenades, but this was refused. But the FBI
men, under separate command, had fewer inhibitions and
police and civilians had to leap for safety as shrapnel from their
grenades zipped through the air and buried itself in the stucco
of neighbouring houses.

A half-hearted attempt was made to evacuate nearby houses
when the firing began. The police were later heavily criticised
for not doing more to ensure the safety of neighbours. Their
reply was that a mass evacuation would have filled the streets
and made it easier for the SLA to break from the house into the
cover of the crowd. As it was, extra police had to be drafted in
to keep back several hundred sightseers, many of whom showed
their hostility to the police by jeering and occasional stone-
throwing.

For a full three-quarters of an hour the gun battle continued
in sporadic but intense bursts. Police and FBI agents fired an
astonishing 5371 rounds of shotgun, rifle and pistol ammunition,
and filled the tiny house with no fewer than eighty-three canisters of CS gas. Incredibly, fire continued to be returned from the
house. Then, at 6.40 pm black smoke was seen coming from a
rear window. The house was on fire.

Critics of the police operation later suggested the house was
deliberately fired with the use of special super-heated gas
canisters. The police in turn claimed the fire was started
either by the accidental ignition of SLA petrol bombs or even
deliberately, perhaps as cover for a desperate break-out, or
even as a last epic act of defiant self-immolation. However it
began, the fire quickly took hold. The SLA faced an instant
decision – surrender or die.

As flames began to shoot from the windows, the leader of
SWAT Team 1 called through the loud-hailer: 'Come on out,
the house is on fire. You won't be harmed.' Suddenly a black
woman appeared at the front door and began to run, screaming

'They held me! They held me!' It was Christine Johnson. She was knocked to the ground by a SWAT man and thrown into a police van. The story she later told was that while the others in the house had been allowed to leave, she had been held hostage. Only when her captors had to turn their attention to the fire did she get her chance to run from the house. She was taken to hospital where she was treated for gunshot wounds and burns. A charge of being an accessory to a felony, namely the harbouring of wanted criminals, was laid against her but later dropped.

In a last desperate attempt to escape the deadly rain of police fire and the now uncontrollable flames, the SLA six hacked their way through the floorboards and crawled into the two-foot space between floor and foundations. DeFreeze, Willie Wolfe and Mizmoon took up positions at ventilator openings through which they could point their guns, though their line of fire was such that they could do little more than shoot high into the air. It was later estimated that some 600 rounds were fired from inside the house, almost all of them from two guns, suggesting that only two of the six fugitives were involved in heavy return fire. Nancy, Camilla and Angela seem to have decided to try to crawl their way out through a ventilation hole. Just before 7 pm, an hour after the shoot-out had begun, Nancy emerged and managed to crawl about ten feet from the house without being seen. Camilla followed her but was spotted by a SWAT marksman, who put a bullet in the centre of her forehead. Her body was pulled back into the floor-space, probably by Angela Atwood. Then Nancy was seen and fired on. Police said she fired one shot back before being riddled by a hail of bullets which tore out her stomach and lungs.

As Nancy and Camilla died, the roof and walls of the house caved in and flames swept into the floor space. The rubber gas masks began to melt on the faces of Donald DeFreeze and his three remaining followers. Minutes later, Angela, Mizmoon and Willie Wolfe were dead from burns and smoke inhalation.

Field-Marshal Cinque, twice wounded at the waist, was the last to die, his mouth pressed to the cool soil to catch the last of the air, a pistol near his right hand and a bullet in his head.

Alone, with the bodies of five dead comrades nearby and the flames sweeping over him, it seemed that Donald DeFreeze fired his last shot to put an end to his own sad, bizarre and baffling life.

Shots continued to be heard from the blazing débris of the house as unused ammunition, some of it still in the belts around the six bodies, exploded in the intense heat. It was 7.30 before all was quiet and a fire-engine was allowed through to douse the flames. Then the police moved in and began to recover the charred, unrecognisable bodies.

At home in Hillsborough, the Hearsts had watched the battle on television. It was nearly midnight before they were called by the police department and told that five bodies had been found. They could be identified only by their dental records and that would take several hours. The Hearsts had to wait another day before knowing whether Patty was among the dead.

Staying with friends at San Diego, Steven Weed had also watched the TV spectacular – later to be nominated for an Emmy award. When it was over, he drove to Los Angeles and arrived at the burned-out house as police sifted through the ruins. Interviewed by newsmen, he was bitterly critical of the SWAT operation: 'Just giving someone a ten-minute choice to surrender is no excuse for an immediate military attack . . . The police have no right to call themselves professionals.' It was an attack which was soon to be taken up by the whole of the Left.

Next day Los Angeles County Coroner Dr Thomas Noguchi identified the dead as DeFreeze, Wolfe, Angela Atwood, Nancy Ling Perry and Mizmoon Soltysik. Noguchi himself called Randolph Hearst to assure him Patty was not among the victims. But even as he did so a sixth body was found under the remains of the house and the Hearsts' agony was prolonged another day before it was identified as that of Camilla Hall. Randolph Hearst issued a brief statement: 'We sympathise and feel sorry for the parents of the people who were in that house. We know what they are going through because we've gone through the same thing.' Later he was much more critical of the police action.

Dr Noguchi supplemented his detailed account of how the

six had died with a 'psychological autopsy' on their motivation. He concluded that they had acted out a 'fanatical fantasy of guerrilla warfare', choosing to die rather than surrender. 'They chose to stay under the floor as the fire burned instead of getting out. And in all my years as a coroner I've never seen this kind of behaviour in the face of live flames.' If they were 'high' said Noguchi, 'it was on revolutionary zeal, not drugs'. Not until the police made their full report four months later did it become clear that Nancy and Camilla at least, far from 'choosing to die', had tried to break out of the burning house, only to be shot dead by the SWAT squad as they emerged.

The police announced a long list of finds in the burned-out house: four automatic rifles including a Browning light machine-gun, six sawn-off shotguns and an array of pistols and assorted ammunition. They later claimed that two of the guns found were traceable to Joseph Remiro and Russell Little and linked with the Foster killing. But, as with their colleagues at Concord four months earlier, their search was astonishingly slapdash. It was left to local souvenir hunters to make important finds: the remains of a passport, a driving licence and a crumpled, charred snapshot of six SLA members posing with rifles and automatic guns before a seven headed cobra poster. One of the six in the picture, lightly disguised in a theatrical wig, was Patty. The finder, a student, sold the picture to *Newsweek* magazine.

For several days the ruined house was besieged by the curious and the pilgrims. A coach tour operator put it on his sightseeing schedule when he found it was more popular than Universal Studios. An enterprising scrap-merchant unscrewed the bath-tub and walked off with it saying he'd sell it as 'the last place Patty Hearst ever had a bath'. On the wall of the next-door house someone aerosol-painted the words '*It took 500 cops*'. Across the whole black community and much of the radical white, there was a surge of sympathy for and defiant solidarity with the four girls and two young men who had died in the most publicised police operation in the city's history. In Los Angeles, San Francisco and Sacramento there were SLA solidarity rallies – the first of their kind. The sympathy the

SLA had vainly craved in its short, violent life it won by the crude and cruel manner of its quick, violent death.

Six days after the shoot-out, Donald DeFreeze was buried by his family in Cleveland. Fifteen hundred sympathisers turned up to give the clenched-fist Black Power salute as his coffin was carried through the streets by members of the militant Sunni Black Muslim sect to which his brother Delano belonged. Delano delivered the oration to a congregation which included Donald's mother and his former wife. 'My fallen brother died for a Nation', he said. 'That Nation might not exist yet, but it will. We must have leaders to guide us to that Nation. My brother was one.' Angela Davis and the Panther leaders were invited to the funeral, but none turned up.

In the Chicago suburb of Lincolnwood, the Rev George F. Hall and his wife Leona sat among the congregation in their own St John's Lutheran Church while seven Lutheran ministers conducted a memorial service to Camilla, who was buried with the skeletal remains of the kitten which was found close to her body.

Angela Atwood's remains were delivered to her parents with an anonymous note scrawled on her identification sheet: 'Not all Californians thought of her as a terrorist. Peace.' Father Joseph Citro, conducting her funeral mass, described Angela as a 'dear, honest, sincere girl,' who, 'like Christ, died for what she believed in'. His eulogy scandalised the local press.

In Santa Rosa, Harold and Marge Ling refused to have a funeral service for Nancy 'because she wouldn't have wanted it – she didn't believe in them'. Instead, they wrote their own simple epitaph to a daughter who 'was always eager to get on with living, always asking questions and seeking answers'.

Often the depth of her curiosity could not be satisfied by the answers she heard.

She was idealistic and firmly believed that problems should be solved and not merely tolerated. She was impetuous and impatient and thus often frustrated because she seldom found the solutions she felt were needed. Intensity, idealism and curiosity are characteristics shared by all that is best in youth, and political activists.

The Nancy we know was compassionate and constantly concerned with the welfare of others. She identified with the oppressed and many times became their advocate. A great deal of her time was given to prisoners and prison reform. Although her own jobs made very little money, she gave a substantial portion of her income to programs for prisoners.

Nancy has been called 'a common criminal'. Common criminals act for their personal gain. We deplore the methods Nancy and the SLA chose to gain their goals but we still feel the goals deserve further scrutiny. Whatever can be said against these methods, Nancy never sought personal gain and ultimately showed herself willing to die for her convictions.

She loved things close to the earth, to be in touch with trees and living things. She was gentle, tender, pliable and therefore often easily hurt. She was capable of great love and needed to be loved. We always loved her and always will. We know she cherished this love, for she told us so many times. In the end, she was willing to sacrifice the closeness of this love to insulate us and the family from her activities. In her last letter to us, written in December, she ended, 'I wish love and happiness to everyone. Stay well and well informed. I love you, Nancy.'

The portrait of the Nancy we saw was one of an intense, serious, compassionate woman, who suffered so from the pain of others that she felt herself driven to take action. This portrait may differ from press accounts, but it is the one we saw.

We wish to thank, from the bottom of our hearts, all of those who have written, called and prayed for Nancy and our family. Hopefully Nancy has now found peace.

Ten months had passed since the formation of the Symbionese Liberation Army, nine since its declaration of war, six since its first combat action, three since Patty's kidnapping. Now at a stroke the cobra had lost six heads and the myth of indestructibility was gone for ever.

8 The Making of Tania Hearst

THE climactic events of 17 May threw up an endless series of questions about the Symbionese Liberation Army, or what was left of it. Above all, where was Patty Hearst?

The last reliable sighting of Patty and the Harrises was that of building contractor Frank Sutter, whose car the trio had hijacked at dawn after dropping Tom Matthews in the Hollywood hills. Sutter was definite and precise about the identity of his hijackers but less so about the exact length of time he spent with them. He told the FBI he had been forced to drive 'all over the place . . . for several hours', but he was in too shocked a state to recall with any clarity just where he went and when. He knows that some time after midday, probably around 1 pm, he was told to drive into Griffith Park, a mile or so west of the Hollywood Bowl, and there told to get out of the car and walk into the trees. He did so, almost resigned to receiving a bullet in his back, and the car roared off with Patty at the wheel. Sutter ran off to sound the alarm but within half an hour, before he had reached the outskirts of the rambling park, he saw his car, empty and abandoned, parked off a lane under the trees.

Had Patty and the Harrises just walked away? If so, where to? Three somewhat unkempt young people, dressed, despite the sweltering Los Angeles weather, in heavy black sweaters, slacks and hiking boots, with knives in their belts and cardboard boxes of guns under their arms, must surely have attracted some attention, the more so since the morning papers carried graphic accounts of the Inglewood shooting and descriptions of the curious trio involved. But if that seems an improbable way to disappear, the alternatives – that they either stole another car or were picked up in Griffith Park by friends – pose more difficulties than they resolve. No other car was reported stolen or hijacked and if they were picked up by friends, how was the rendezvous arranged? More important, since the whereabouts of all other known members of the SLA are accounted for at that time, where did these new friends spring from?

There were the reports that Patty did spend some time at the house in Compton that day, but the reports are flawed. Mrs Carr, in informing the police of the presence in her daughter's house of 'white girls with guns', is said to have identified Patty from a police photograph. But Mrs Carr had stayed at the house barely long enough to confirm her grandchildren's accounts of strange occurrences. By her own account she had only glimpsed the white girls, and was probably more impressed by their dress and weaponry than by their faces.

Another more detailed indentification was given by James Johnson who was in the house when the SLA party arrived, and says he was paid $30 by DeFreeze to help unload guns and ammunition from the two vans. He later told reporters that the party consisted of 'five white chicks, one white guy and two black dudes'. One of the girls, he claimed, told him she was Patty Hearst and added: 'They'll have to kill me before I go back.' According to Johnson's account, she had wanted to stay in the house, but 'I think some brothers tipped 'em off that the cops were on to them and that's why they got Patty out of there – you know, their love for her.' Two black men drove up to the house in a van, says Johnson, and Patty walked outside and got in with them and drove off. 'They didn't say where they were going – they were just getting away from the heat.' Johnson put Patty's departure at about 3.30 pm – barely two hours before the fatal siege began.

But his story, although taken seriously by the FBI, should

again almost certainly be discounted. Patty could not have arrived with De Freeze: she was in the back of a van with
Tom Matthews at the time, desperately trying to shake off
police pursuit after the Inglewood fiasco. All other witnesses
say there were four white girls in the SLA party, not five, and
one black man, not two. And it is implausible that Patty joined
the group later in the day. If she abandoned Frank Sutter's car
in Griffith Park between 1.0 and 1.30 pm, how would she
travel the ten miles across the centre of Los Angeles to the
black ghetto of Compton? And what would the Harrises be
doing in the meantime? How would she know where DeFreeze's
party was staying? And knowing that the trail of hijacked cars
must be hot, would she have risked leading the police to the
rest of the guerrilla band? No, Patty was not at Compton.

During the week following the shoot-out, reported sightings
of Patty and the Harrises flooded into police and FBI offices
at the staggering rate of two hundred a day. Some were taken
very seriously. On the Sunday night, two days after the fire
and within hours of the public announcement that the sixth
body found was that of Camilla Hall, a Los Angeles landlady
reported that a girl resembling Patty had walked into her
apartment house just before midnight and offered $500 for a
room for twenty-four hours. Told that there was no room available, the girl had summoned two companions who were waiting on the stairs. The girl resembling Patty had pointed 'a
big black gun' at her and asked 'Do you want to die?' while one
of her companions – the landlady thought he was 'a black
man' – slashed at her with a knife, ripping her dress. When she
started screaming the three fled in 'a red car with a black top'.
The landlady called the police and later identified Patty from
police pictures.

The following night an eighty-three-year-old retired US army
sergeant, William Walls, was watching television in his tiny,
shack-like home in remote Placerita Canyon near the San
Fernando Valley when, at about 7.30 pm, three people he later
identified as Patty and Emily and Bill Harris drove up to his
home in a red Chevrolet with a black top, said they were lost
and asked if they could spend the night at his home. Mr Walls

said he didn't have enough room, so they asked him for directions to reach Los Angeles by minor roads, avoiding the freeway. The trio were polite, didn't offer any money, and drove away with the Harrises in the front seats and Patty in the back. Minutes later Mr Walls, who thought he recognised their faces from newspaper and television photographs, called the police. The canyon was quickly cordoned off, but there was no sign of the red car with a black top, nor of Patty Hearst and her comrades.

For the Hearst family in Hillsborough, their immense relief that Patty had somehow missed being burned to death with her captors was tempered by a chilling realisation that the theory of duress to which they had clung so long was becoming progressively harder to maintain. Patty the unwilling prisoner of Emily and Bill Harris? Hardly. The same doubts evidently entered the minds of FBI and police chiefs. From now on, Patty would no longer be given the benefit of the doubt.

Two days after the shoot-out the FBI branded Patty, along with the Harrises, as 'armed and dangerous fugitives', indicting her on firearms charges in connection with the Inglewood shooting. Three days later, as if to outdo the federal agency, the District-Attorney filed nineteen State charges against Patty, including five charges of assault with intent to commit murder, four of assault with a deadly weapon, four of robbery, three of unlawfully taking a vehicle, one of simple kidnapping (Matthews) and one of kidnapping for the purpose of robbery (Sutter). The last charge alone carried a life sentence on conviction. Some of the charges – assault to commit murder, for instance, which related to the burst of shooting at Inglewood and the alleged incident with the Los Angeles landlady – seemed grossly over-reactive, but District-Attorney Joseph P. Busch unwittingly made it clear why the State authorities were throwing the book at Patty. 'The seriousness of the charges we have filed,' he told the press 'and the greater number we have filed would make it more profitable to go to trial on our case before the FBI's.' But in this continuing game of rivalries the FBI still had its trump card to play. A few days later the federal grand jury which had been investigating the Hibernia bank robbery in San Francisco – for which, until now, Patty had been wanted only as a 'material witness' – indicted her for armed robbery on a count that could put her in jail for thirty-five years. Having thus spelt out what was in store for her if she was found, both State and federal agencies urged her to be sensible and give herself up.

Randolph Hearst, furious at the ineptness of an onslaught which clearly reflected the FBI's sense of humiliation at the SLA's hands, told newsmen at another of his Hillsborough press conferences that he didn't believe that Patty was 'going to give herself up just to come home and be carted off to jail'. Patty had done 'nothing except fire a gun'. It was doubtful that she was in the bank of her own free will. 'I hope the police still realise that she is a kidnap victim.' Then, indicating that he thought of the Harrises rather than Patty as dictating policy, he went on, 'I just hope that William and Emily Harris, who are not stupid people, have enough sense, and that they don't get in another shoot-out and force police to kill them.' Catherine Hearst added a tearful reminder that her daughter was still 'a victim of thought control by terrorists'. Then Patty's sisters, Vicki and Anne, went on television with an appeal. Vicki warned, 'The police and FBI are not that sympathetic any more. They've taken a lot of trash from you guys.' Anne told Patty, 'If you really feel the SLA is your thing, I don't think you should get yourself killed. Everyone wants to see what you have to say. If you are killed, it would be a terrible waste.'

Emily Harris's father, Frederick Schwartz, also appealed to the fugitives, picking up Anne Hearst's theme of 'live and tell': 'Your cause whatever it is, is even this minute dying. The only way to revive it for whatever noble ideas it possesses is for you to live . . . Everyone knows you each have God-given talents, high ideals and the kind of dedication so badly needed to solve the social problems of this country. If you live, we will all benefit.'

The same message came from a group of Emily's former schoolfriends in Chicago: 'Em – many of your friends want you to know we're thinking of you and care for your safety. You cannot effectively continue with your cause while a fugitive.

Live, Em – your cause will not be best served by another 54th and Compton.'

The response came, not from Patty, Emily and Bill but from District-Attorney Busch: 'We would hope they would surrender, but we are in no position to offer them any kind of deal.' And all over the country the FBI's 'Wanted' poster went up, with its incongruous mug-shots and descriptions of William ('wears Fu Manchu type mustache'), Emily ('natural food faddist, exercises by jogging, swimming and bicycle riding') and Patty ('may wear wigs, including Afro-style . . . last seen wearing black sweater, plaid slacks, brown hiking boots and carrying a knife in her belt . . . CONSIDERED ARMED AND VERY DANGEROUS').

No fewer than 200 FBI agents and sixty Los Angeles policemen were assigned full-time to the hunt for the rump of the SLA. Every reported sighting was checked out. For a week or more there were raids on ranches and caves in the hills and canyons, using police helicopters for air surveillance. On 29 May one policeman was killed and three injured when a helicopter crashed over a remote part of the San Fernando Valley, an incident which sparked off a wild rumour that the SLA trio, cornered in some wilderness hideout, had shot it down. Another rumour had it that the trio planned to cross into the rugged Baja peninsula to join Mexican revolutionaries of the 23rd of September League who were believed to be hiding out in the mountains. Both the Mexican and the Canadian borders were closely watched.

As the search went on, so too did the arguments. The families of Willie Wolfe and Angela Atwood hired a team of independent investigators, including Pentagon Papers attorney Leonard Weinglas, to enquire into the LAPD's tactics at the shoot-out. The investigators' report accused the police of deliberately setting fire to the house and charged that 'although firemen were on the scene more than an hour before the house caught fire, members of the fire department were threatened with arrest by police as they attempted to advance to the house to extinguish the blaze'. The American Civil Liberties Union also criticised the police for failing to give adequate warning, using

an 'unwise amount of force', failing to evacuate the neighbourhood and above all, failing to allow an escape path for SLA
members who wanted to give themselves up. The city council's
response to all this was to pass a resolution praising 'police high
command and all personnel for an outstanding demonstration
of courage and efficiency in freeing this city and the nation of
an unconscionable reign of terror imposed by wanton, mis-
guided and merciless revolutionaries'. More sinisterly, the
California Senate Sub-committee on Civil Disorders – heir of
the disbanded Sub-committee on Un-American Activities –
recommended that the best preventive measure against SLA-
type actions was to place radical political groups under constant
surveillance by the appointment in each locality of 'a neighbourhood source of reliable information regarding suspect persons
or unusual happenings'.

California's fragmented Left continued to argue and agonise
over the SLA. A conference of thirty representatives from
nearly as many Left-wing organisations concluded that 'while
the SLA was not a typical Leftist movement, while its violent
tactics violated the codes of current activists, and while it made
revolution a media event, its murdered members serve to in-
spire an upsurge on the Left, raising consciousness and increas-
ing commitment'. But there were dissenters from this line. One
young man flayed 'those noodle-brains who think that the SLA
is the best thing since Jesus Christ', adding that the only simi-
larity was that 'like Jesus, the SLA died for other people's
fantasies'. Articulating the orthodox Left's view that the SLA
had done the radical cause more harm than good, he went on:

The moronic politics and inflated utterances of the self-
styled generals was only out-grossed by their acts and eventual suicide. The only effect of all that can be to set back the
cause of social justice another hundred years. Everybody who
disagreed with them was either a 'pig' or a 'fascist' and slated
for death without trial or explanation. The SLA had become
the pigs they hated.

Romantics are a dime a dozen. Berkeley politics are so
divorced from reality these days that anybody jerking off in

public will be taken for a true revolutionary if he shouts 'Power to the People' while he's doing it . . . Rage is useless, enraged people are powerless. Rage makes clear thinking and clear tactics impossible.

But Leftist opposition to the SLA had yet more rage to contend with. At the end of May, the long-quiescent Weather Underground surfaced to bomb Attorney-General Evelle Younger's office and to announce: 'We do this on the occasion of the most recent act of terrorism unleashed by the Government against six freedom-fighters from the Symbionese Liberation Army.' It was Bernadine Dorhn's salute not only to the SLA dead but also to the sisters and brother who had followed her into hiding.

Another shadowy body emerged briefly with its own message of solidarity. On 25 May Berkeley's KPFA radio received a taped communiqué from the Black Liberation Army and its 'General Field-Marshal Cabrella'. The tape claimed that 'an emergency meeting held after the events in Los Angeles' had resulted in the merging of the 'Federated Forces of the Symbionese Liberation Army' with a new 'united front of urban guerrilla organisations'. It was the same empty bombast over again, but the tape concluded with an 'ode to six slain soldiers' which struck a note of authenticity. Nine months earlier the Black Liberation Army had assured the new-born SLA of its sympathy for the notion of a united 'Symbionese War Council' but had warily held back from actually joining. Now the BLA told the dead Nancy, Angela, Mizmoon, Camilla and Willie Wolfe,

We watched you as America's children, standing on the outer perimeter of our base camp. We wondered if you would ever come and join us to sit around the campfire to share the pains and the sorrow of revolution – and then one night you approached us. We knew not whether to trust you for you bore the trappings of white skin. Would you fail to pick up your comrades and wash their painful wounds? Would you leave your comrades in the urban war zone and then run safely back to suburbia? We mourn for you now but we know that you are one of us and are with us. Our doubts prevented us from embracing you as comrades, but your courageous display of comradeship has united us for ever . . . We mourn your death but we smile with joy, knowing that America's children have come of age.

The communiqué contained a message to Tania, Bill and Emily: 'Regroup, regroup, do nothing in haste – we will unite in time'. And it added: 'We love you Tania. We're moving on to higher ground.'

It was probably with their old contacts from the BLA that Patty and the Harrises began their new life underground.

At 6.30 on the morning of 7 June, three weeks after Patty, Emily and Bill left Frank Sutter in Griffith Park, an anonymous caller telephoned the early morning disc jockey on Los Angeles radio station KPFK and said there was a new SLA tape under a mattress in the alley behind the station.

The cassette was found, and a small army of newsmen was summoned to hear it. On the tape, which was broadcast at noon, were the voices of Field-Marshal Cinque's successor, General Tico, followed by Yolande and Tania. Each of the carefully constructed speeches was defiant to the last: three final fist-shaking testimonies by which the world would remember the astonishing phenomenon of what had once been the Symbionese Liberation Army.

The tape began with the voice of William Harris.

To those who would bear the hopes and future of our people, let the voice of their guns express the words of freedom. Greetings to the people: The Black Liberation Army, the United People's Army, the Black Guerrilla Family, the Weather Underground and all freedom fighters of the United Symbionese Federation and the New World Liberation Front.

This is Tico speaking. Yolande, Tania and I extend profound feelings of revolutionary love and solidarity to General

Field-Marshal Cabrella and all soldiers of the United People's Liberation Army; to the B-team commander and all elements of the anti-aircraft forces of the SLA; to Combat Unit 4 of the Black Liberation Army; to comrade Martin Sostre and all other comrade brothers and sisters in America's concentration camps.

To our beloved comrades-in-arms, Osceola and Bo, we echo the words you have often left us with: 'A Luca Continua... Venceremos.'

We have come together in many different cells, squads and military-political units. We have taken many different meaningful names. But we are not hung up on names for, as comrades-in-arms, we are one in our struggle for freedom. The determination to eliminate our common enemy by force of arms has united us. To our comrade sisters and brothers of the Black Liberation Army and all other fighters, let it be known that the Malcolm X Combat Unit of the Symbionese Liberation Army proudly takes up the banner of the New World Liberation Front.

Then followed an account of how and why the 'Malcolm X combat unit' – Patty, Bill and Emily – had left San Francisco for Los Angeles.

The Malcolm X Combat Unit of the Symbionese Liberation Army left the San Francisco Bay Area in a successful effort to break a massive pig encirclement. It had become clear from intelligence reports from other SLA elements and from the people in the community that the pigs were preparing to trap us on the San Francisco peninsula. We knew there was a great risk in setting up a base of operations in San Francisco, which is a natural defile, a trap. The area was very small, surrounded by water and with limited choices for breaking a major encirclement. However, we accepted this potentially dangerous condition because we saw the importance of making solid contacts in the oppressed communities of this city. We considered ourselves to be an underground unit; however, the majority of our unit's members moved about freely, and in the five months we were there, we made many good contacts.

We decided to move our base of operations to Southern California, concentrating on the Greater Los Angeles area with its vast oppressed communities and more favourable terrain. In April, the War Council dispatched an intelligence and reconnaissance team to Los Angeles. Its mission: to make some additional contacts and survey the area. Based on the favourable results of this mission and the concentration of pig activity in the San Francisco Bay Area, our unit slipped out of San Francisco and into Los Angeles on May Day, 1974.

Then came Harris's account – an outright denial – of the shoplifting incident which had given away the SLA's presence in Los Angeles.

On Thursday, May 16, 1974, three members of the Malcolm X Combat Unit of the SLA were sent out to buy a number of items needed by the unit. At Mel's Sporting Goods Store in Inglewood a pig-agent clerk named Tony Shepard, attempting to show his allegiance to his reactionary white bosses, falsely accused me of shoplifting. It was impossible to allow a verifying search by a store security guard because I was armed, and therefore we were forced to fight our way out of the situation.

The pigs originally said that a 49 cent pair of socks was stolen, and that this was what caused the shootout at the store. The people found this very difficult to believe when it was pointed out that we had already purchased over $30 worth of heavy wool socks and other items. This, apparently, became increasingly confusing to the pigs, who later charged that an ammunition bandolier was the item taken, supposedly to make the accusation more believable.

The policy of the Symbionese Liberation Army has always been to avoid shoplifting because of the heavy risk involved to the whole unit. We cannot afford to have soldiers busted on humbug charges. However, we realise that the combat and support elements run a great risk of being jammed whenever we move about above ground. The most unfortunate aspect of this situation was that the pigs then learned that SLA elements were in the Los Angeles area. It appears that even with this knowledge, the pigs would not have located our comrades if a collaborator named Mary Carr had not snitched to the enemy.

Harris went on to give the SLA's version of what had happened at Compton.

On Friday, May 17, 1974, a CIA-directed force of FBI agents, Los Angeles City, County and California State pigs, with air support and reserve assistance from the United States Marine Corps and the National Guard, encircled elements of the Malcolm X Combat Unit of the Symbionese Liberation Army. The result of the encirclement was that the people witnessed on live television the burning to death of six of their most beautiful and courageous freedom-fighters by cowardly, fascist insects. In most cases when an urban guerilla unit is encircled by the enemy, it can expect to take great losses, especially if the enemy has time to mobilise a massive force.

Our six comrades were not on a suicide mission, as the pigs would have us believe. They were attempting to break a battalion-sized encirclement. By looking at the diagrams of where their bodies were found, it is clear that they had split into two teams, moved to opposite sides of the rear of the house and were preparing to move out of the house by force. The heavy automatic weapons fired from the front of the house was a diversionary tactic to force the pigs to concentrate some of their forces in the front. The two dynamite-loaded pipe bombs were to be used as fragmentation grenades to clear a path through the cringing pigs who had started the blaze by firing incendiary grenades into the house.

Cin, Fahizah, Zoya, Cujo, Gelina and Gabi died of smoke inhalation and burns before they could get outside. The pigs want us to believe that the fire was started by the SLA; that it was caused by SLA molotov cocktails; or by accident from

pig tear-gas grenades. This is pig-shit. The SWAT squad, FBI
and LAPD would have had to go into the house themselves
to clear it out. They showed their true cowardice by using
incendiary grenades to cause the fire that killed our comrades.

For those who don't know, incendiary grenades burn at
such an incredible temperature that they melt steel and
armour plate in a matter of seconds and are impossible to
extinguish.

The pigs want the people to believe that the bad-ass tactics
of the SLA guerillas drove the fascists to use such barbaric
force. But we say that the SLA is a reaction to fascism. The
SLA uses automatic weapons and home-made bombs because
the pigs have automatic weapons, artillery and hydrogen
bombs.

Then Harris turned to a passionate defence of DeFreeze,
brushing aside the strong indications that he had killed himself
and scornfully repudiating the suggestion, tentatively advanced
for the first time by the 'Citizens Research and Investigation
Committee' at the end of May, that he had once been in the pay
of the Los Angeles police. DeFreeze, it seems, had successfully
kept his guilty secret from his comrades.

The pigs want the people to believe that General Field-
Marshal Cinque Mtume committed suicide. To this absurdity,
the SLA responds by quoting our beloved comrade brother.
He often said: 'We must not fear death, for to fear death is
to put our fear of pig terror before our love of the children
and the people's struggle for freedom.' The pigs have historically focused on eliminating black leaders. Many have been
murdered and imprisoned in America's concentration camps.

For over a year, the pigs couldn't find Cin to murder him,
so they attempted to isolate him from the people with pig
propaganda. First they worked on the most blatantly racist
whites with their traditional 'crazy-black-nigger, escaped-
convict-rapist' routine. Next, we learned that Cin was a plum
wine alcoholic. This obviously was the white racist, liberal
answer to the logic that a black revolutionary leader could

order and assist in the assassination of a jive-assed, pig-agent school superintendent.

It followed that the white supremacists and bourgeois black elements of the revolutionary Left so-called leadership would be pimped with ridiculous tales of links between the SLA and the CIA – that Cin was and had been a paid informer for the Los Angeles Police Department and the California Attorney-General's office. If this were true, we dare these fools and collaborators to explain Cin's reward for his deeds – a life term in California's concentration camps.

White, sickeningly liberal, paranoid conspiracy freaks and spaced-out counter-culture dope fiends proved their naïveté and amateurish research skills as they rambled on and on and on about the California Department of Corrections. Bizarre stories about Cin having been programmed and electrodes implanted in his brain while at Vacaville began to appear in the so-called underground press. [Apparently a reference to a Berkeley student newssheet which had commented on Vacaville's 'behaviour modification' experiments and suggested DeFreeze might be the product of one such experiment which had gone wrong.]

Cinque Mtume: the name means 'Fifth Prophet'. Cin was indeed a prophet. The pigs would have the people believe that Cin was just, as they would say, another dumb nigger. They continually attempted to undermine his leadership by propagandising that Cin was being fronted off by whites; that he wasn't smart enough to be the brains behind the planning and execution of the successful SLA actions.

To this display of racism we say, go into the black community and ask the people if Cinque Mtume was not a prophet. Ask the people if they think he was being used by whites. The people know that a black man in America does not need conscious whites to push him into leading a revolution. Racists cannot believe that middle and upper-middle class whites and a daughter of a super-fascist ruling-class family would ever have reason to follow the lead of a beautiful black genius, revolutionary warrior, and give their lives for the people.

THE MAKING OF TANIA HEARST

THE MAKING OF TANIA HEARST   201

Sick-assed racists would have us believe that white women who follow the lead of black revolutionaries are only mindless cunts enslaved by gigantic black penises. The cringing pigs who faced the fire-power of Gelina, Gabi, Fahizah, and Zoya know much better.

Racists believe that it is impossible for white men to denounce white racism and follow the revolutionary leadership of black men, but the SLA proved this theory to be a sick delusion. Cinque Mtume, himself, was the spirit of Frederick Douglass, Gabriel Process, Denmark Veese, Marcus Garvey, the Scottsborough Boys, Medgar Evers, William E. Burhardt DeBois, Malcolm X, Martin Luther King, Emmett Till, little Bobby Hutton, Fred Hampton, L. B. Barkley, Jonathan and George L. Jackson, Mark Essex and every other black freedom fighter who came before him.

To racist slander, the SLA and all the people say: 'Death to the fascist insect that preys upon the life of the people.'

And now, after our comrade brother fought valiantly against a battalion of pigs – a battle witnessed by millions – these same chicken-shit pigs are trying to have us believe that General Field-Marshal of the Symbionese Liberation Army Cinque Mtume killed himself. Cin was so determined to kill pigs that as long as his heart was beating and there was any air in his lungs at all, he would fight, even if his only weapon was his body. We all know that revolutionaries do not kill themselves. Revolutionaries kill the enemy.

Cin was the baddest member of the SLA and therefore our leader. Our five white comrades who died with him were among his students and had learned well. They, too, showed incredible determination and courage. Cujo, Gelina, Fahizah, Zoya and Gabi did not commit suicide, as the pigs would have us believe. Pigs tell us it is suicidal for whites to join blacks and other oppressed people in making revolution. To this 'oinking' we say, it is suicidal for the ruling class and all its pig agents to believe that they can continue to oppress, exploit, murder and imprison an undivided revolutionary army of the people. White Americans who follow the example of our beautiful comrades and join the fight for the freedom of all oppressed people will not do so because they wish to die, but because they wish to be free.

And so to his warning peroration:

The pigs boast that they have broken the back of the Symbionese Liberation Army. But to do this the pigs would have to break the back of the people. The military-political leader of the SLA and five top cadres have been killed by the fascists. However, the SLA is not dead and will not die as long as there is one living, fighting member of any oppressed class, race, sex or group left on the face of this earth. The pigs have won a battle, but the war of the flea is not over. As our dear comrade Ho Chi Minh once wrote from an imperialist prison, 'Today the locust fights the elephant, but tomorrow the elephant will be disembowelled.'

Then it was Emily's turn. Her cold, curiously monotonous voice pressed home the relentless message that the fight would go on, that the battle of Compton would prove a beginning, not an end.

Greetings and profound love to the people, to all comrades-in-arms, to all comrades in concentration camps in fascist America, and to all the children. This is Yolande speaking.

When we say revolution, we do not use the word loosely. By revolution we mean the violent fight for freedom – freedom that can be gained in no other way than by fighting. People do not fight because they enjoy it or because they relish the thought of their own death or the deaths of their beloved comrades. They fight to survive, because they understand the violence of fascism; and that violence means genocidal death at the hands of dictators who massed 500 pigs, armed with military weapons, fragmentary grenades and incendiary grenades, to burn six people to death. Dictators who have imprisoned over 22,000 brothers and sisters in the State of California alone. Dictators who take jobs away from those who are begging to work. Dictators who take food from the mouths of those who are starving. Dictators who take joy from the hearts of those who love the people.

The military-industrial state of the ruling class can only survive through repression. These fascist dogs must destroy truth in the minds of the people to keep them pacified. They must make people afraid so that they'll do nothing. They must make people feel isolated from each other and power-less.

Fascism tries to do all these things through the brutal violence of the military police forces, the lurking big-brother presence of the FBI, CIA and their computer files, through media propaganda. Fascism tries to tell us we are fools to resist, because in the end we will be destroyed.

If we were only six people, they would be correct, for they can destroy the lives of six, or nine, or even one hundred people. But the truth the pigs try so desperately to repress is one the people are coming to understand only too well. People are ridding themselves of the bourgeois desire to lead a long life, and instead wish to fight for a better, more human life. Yes, repression breeds resistance. It is proven to be true as each day goes by, as dark eyes grow darker with hate, and strong muscles grow stronger with age, and cold steel grows colder in the firm grip of a hand that loves the people.

We must face the inevitable truth that repression will grow more intense as the power-hungry pigs see their grip slipping. Whites in this country have historically had a tend-ency to back off when repression intensified, feeling they could escape the vicious tentacles. For this reason, black, brown, Asian and Indian brothers and sisters have not trusted whites, feeling that they would desert the fight as it was just beginning in order to save their own skin. These brothers and sisters were often proven correct. That is why we say anyone who loves freedom must prove this love through action, not words. And only after they have fought can they speak.

So we are freedom fighters. We may be murdered, but whether we live or die, the day is close at hand when the people will join together in an army because of the wish to survive on their own terms, and the people will change the course of history through their courage and determination. To all those whose fear is stronger than their hatred of the pig, I must say that the freedom fighters do not bring repression to your door. The fascist pig is responsible for this, and soon even those of you with white skins will lose your privileges.

The pig will no longer knock and be polite. He will shoot to kill. He will burn and rape. He will imprison and starve. He does this already in the ghettos of this country, and will expand his efforts to stay in his greed-filled position of power. And if people wish to survive, they will have to defend themselves with as much rage as the pigs would use against them. Only in this way can the people in this country avoid the mass genocide that occurred to Jews in Germany and Leftists in Chile.

All these things have been said before, but I will continue to say them until the reality is so clear we no longer need to repeat the words. That will be the day when our mind accepts what we see with our eyes.

To those who have attempted to express their love for us by calling for our surrender, we say we must express our feelings of love only by continuing the fight. We renounce our class and race privilege, so that we love no individual more than we love freedom. The fight has cost us of the SLA eight comrades: six dead, and two in concentration camps, as well as the death and imprisonment of our comrades-in-arms of the BLA, the BGF and the Weather Underground.

We clearly understand that the reality of revolution will include death and imprisonment, suffering and violence, as well as victory. The price is high, but we accepted this reality when we picked up the gun for the first time and nodded a yes to freedom, to love, to living. Because we must endure the suffering does not mean we have any doubt in the beauty of the victory.

Our comrades died the way they chose to live – fighting courageously. They did not compromise to the hundreds of insects crawling the community who resorted to burning them to death rather than facing in battle the ruthless strength and courage of freedom fighters. Fifty-fourth Street is not an end, but a beginning. People are gathering on the street. They are feeling the strength of their own bodies. They are clearing the fear and blind ignorance from their eyes. Cinque, Fahizah, Zoya, Cujo, Gelina and Gabi conquered the fear and will never die in the minds of those who see the monster and know that he will be destroyed.

All comrades, dead and alive, in prison and out, underground and on the streets, are calling on all the people to conquer fear and join the battle, realising what can happen when 500 pigs surround a house, and then are surrounded by 50, or 100, or 500 irate niggers firing from their houses, alleyways, treetops and walls with a straight and fearless shot to bring down the helicopter, the SWAT squad, the LAPD, the FBI, the neighbourhood snitch. Consider the day when the pig won't even enter the communities of the armed people. We've got to make the pig fear for his life, because he knows every eye behind every curtain in the ghettos, barrios and poor communities is sighting down the barrel of a piece, ready to pull the trigger at any moment.

There's been a lot of talk about wasted lives, referring to the six dead bodies of our comrades, and to Tania, Tico and myself. The ironies of racist, fascist America are once again reflected with sickening reminder. There are no editorials written for the wasted lives of the brothers and sisters daily gunned down in the streets and prisons. The present uproar of white America over the fate of Patty Hearst was barely a murmur as hundreds of young men, mostly black and brown, went off to die in Vietnam.

We of the SLA hate the historical reality that requires young people to struggle to survive and to die violent deaths. We hate the reality in this country that murdered our six comrade sisters and brothers and daily continues to murder throughout the world. Because we hate this reality we must fight to destroy it by any means necessary. Yes, history might be different if they had lived, but revolution is not made by saying 'if only'. We do know that the lives of revolutionaries will never be wasted.

Right now there are men and women, young and old, black, brown, Asian, Indian and white who are filled with the fighting spirit of King, of Malcolm, of George, of Cinque, of your mothers, fathers, sisters and brothers who have died at the hands of the pig. And these are a new breed of the baddest motherfuckers alive. Yes, we hate the pig, and we are at war with the pig, and we will kill the pig as violently as he has killed comrades of ours for centuries. We will do this because we love the people we are lucky enough to know; and we love the people we will never know: the beautiful babies, the angry young men and women, the understanding mothers and fathers who have seen the rising tide for as long as they have been alive.

And finally, an epitaph on her own past life and that of her comrades.

Our past as middle-class white Americans was meaningless. It was truly wasted potential, filled with desperate pessimism that could feel the emptiness of capitalist America even before we could understand it. Our lives now are not easy or full of joy. We may die. But our lives are real, because we see the truth and the future. Right now the people are igniting the spark for the great prairie fire, and the fire-fighters will soon be helpless against the freedom fighters because the flames will be far too hot and deadly for their weak wills to endure, and their evil spirit will die with them in the ashes.

Once again, my love to all the comrades.

The voice stopped. There was a long pause. The SLA had not yet lost its sense of the dramatic. Then, at last, the voice of Patty, hard and brittle as the barrel of a gun. Patty on her love, her comrades, her teacher; on renouncing her class privilege; on the impossibility of ever again returning to 'the pig Hearsts'.

Greetings to the people. This is Tania. I want to talk about the way I knew our six murdered comrades because the fascist pig media has, of course, been painting a typically distorted picture of these beautiful sisters and brothers.

Cujo [Willie Wolfe] was the gentlest, most beautiful man I've ever known. He taught me the truth as he learned it from the beautiful brothers in California's concentration camps. We loved each other so much, and his love for the people was so deep that he was willing to give his life for them.

The name Cujo means 'unconquerable'. It was the perfect name for him. Cujo conquered life as well as death by facing and fighting them. Neither Cujo or I had ever loved an individual the way we loved each other, probably because our relationship wasn't based on bourgeois, fucked-up values, attitudes and goals. Our relationship's foundation was our commitment to the struggle and our love for the people. It's because of this that I still feel strong and determined to fight.

I was ripped off by the pigs when they murdered Cujo, ripped off in the same way that thousands of sisters and brothers in this fascist country have been ripped off of people they love. We mourn together, and the sound of gunfire becomes sweeter.

Gelina [Angela Atwood] was beautiful. Fire and joy. She exploded with the desire to kill the pigs. She wrote poetry – some of it on the walls of Golden Gate, all of it in the LA pig files now – that expresses how she felt. She loved the people more than her love for any one person or material comfort, and she never let her mind rest from the strategies that are the blood of revolution. Gelina would have yelled 'Fire Power to the People' if there wasn't the need to whisper the words of revolution. We laughed and cried and struggled together. She taught me how to fight the enemy within through her constant struggle with bourgeois conditioning.

Gabi [Camilla Hall] crouched low with her ass to the ground. She practised until her shotgun was an extension of her right and left arms, an impulse, a tool of survival. She understood the evil in the heart of the pig and took the only road that could demoralise, defeat and destroy him. She loved to touch people with a strong – not delicate – embrace. Gabi

taught me the patience and discipline necessary for survival
and victory.

Zoya [Patricia 'Mizmoon' Soltysik] wanted to give meaning to her name, and on her birthday she did. Zoya, female
guerilla, perfect love and perfect hate reflected in stone-cold
eyes. She moved viciously and with caution, understanding
the peril of the smallest mistake. She taught me, 'Keep your
ass down and be bad.'

Fahizah [Nancy Ling Perry] was a beautiful sister who
didn't talk much but who was the teacher of many by her
righteous example. She, more than any other, had come to
understand and conquer the putrid disease of bourgeois
mentality. She proved often that she was unwilling to compromise with the enemy because of her intense love for
freedom. Fahizah taught me the perils of hesitation – to
shoot first and make sure the pig is dead before splitting. She
was wise and bad, and I'll always love her.

Cinque [Donald DeFreeze] loved the people with tenderness and respect. They listened to him when he talked because
they knew that his love reflected the truth and the future.
Cin knew that to live was to shoot straight. He longed to be
with his black sisters and brothers, but at the same time he
wanted to prove to black people that white freedom fighters
are comrades-in-arms. Cinque was in a race with time, believing that every minute must be another step forward in
the fight to save the children. He taught me virtually everything imaginable, but wasn't liberal with us. He'd kick our
asses if we didn't hop over a fence fast enough or keep our
asses down while practicing. Most importantly, he taught me
how to show my love for the people. He helped me see that
it's not how long you live that's important, it's how we
live; what we decide to do with our lives. On February 4th
Cinque Mtume saved my life.

The Malcolm X Combat Unit of the SLA was a leadership
training cell, under the personal command of General
Field-Marshal Cinque. General Tico was his second in command. Everything we did was directed toward our development as leaders and advisors to other units. All of us were

prepared to function on our own if necessary until we connected with other combat units. The idea that we are leaderless is absurd as long as any SLA elements are alive and operating under the command of our General Field-Marshal.

It's hard to explain what it was like watching our comrades die, murdered by pig incendiary grenades. A battalion of pigs facing a fire-team of guerrillas, and the only way they could defeat them was to burn them alive. It made me mad to see the pigs looking at our comrades' weapons – to see them holding Cujo's .45 and his watch which was still ticking. He would have laughed at that. There is no surrender. No one in that house was suicidal – just determined and full of love.

It was beautiful to hear Gabi's father. He understands. Gabi loved her father and I know that much of her strength came from the support he gave her. What a difference between the parents of Gabi and Cujo, and my parents. One day, just before making the last tape, Cujo and I were talking about the way my parents were fucking me over. He said that his parents were still his parents because they had never betrayed him, but my 'parents' were really Malcolm X and Assata Shakur. I'll never betray my 'parents'.

The pigs probably have the little old man monkey that Cujo wore around his neck. He gave me the little stone face one night.

I know that the pigs are proud of themselves. They've killed another black leader. In typical pig fashion they have said that Cinque committed suicide. What horseshit! Cin committed suicide the same way that Malcolm, King, Bobby, Fred, Jonathan and George did. But no matter how many leaders are killed, the pig can't kill their ideals.

I learned a lot from Cin and the comrades that died in that fire, and I'm still learning from them. They live on in the hearts and minds of millions of people in fascist America. The pig's actions that Friday evening showed just how scared they really are. They would have burned and bombed that entire neighbourhood to murder six guerrillas.

The SLA terrifies the pigs because it calls all oppressed

people in this country to arms to fight in a united front to overthrow the fascist dictatorship. The pigs think they can deal with a handful of revolutionaries, but they know they can't defeat the incredible power which the people, once united, represent.

It's for this reason that we get to see – live and in colour – the terrorist tactics of the pigs. The pigs saying 'you're next'. This kind of display, however, only serves to raise the people's consciousness and makes it easier for our comrade sisters and brothers throughout the country to connect. I died in that fire on 54th Street, but out of the ashes I was reborn. I know what I have to do. Our comrades didn't die in vain. The pig lies about the advisability of surrender have only made me more determined. I renounced my class privilege when Cin and Cujo gave me the name Tania. While I have no death wish, I have never been afraid of death. For this reason, the brainwash/duress theory of the Pig Hearsts has always amused me.

Life is very precious to me, but I have no delusions that going to prison will keep me alive. I would never choose to live the rest of my life surrounded by pigs like the Hearsts. I want to see our comrades in this country's concentration camps, but on our terms as stated in our Revolutionary Declaration of War, not on the pigs' terms.

Patria o muerte . . . Venceremos! Death to the fascist insect that preys upon the life of the people.

And then the silence. Only four months had passed since Patty's kidnapping. Now the rest of 1974, the remaining seven months of the SLA's 'Year of the Soldier', would dribble away without further sight or sound of Tania and her two comrades in arms.

There were false alarms: phoney communiqués, more police invasions of houses which proved empty, reported sightings in Chicago, Miami, Idaho, Mexico, Guatemala. And there were stories: the trio had taken a fishing boat to Honduras, were hiding in a cave in the grounds of Hearst Castle, had been kidnapped by rival revolutionaries, were dead.

A mood of exhausted resignation began to grip the Hearst family. The ceaseless telephone calls, the shanty-town encampment of newsmen on their doorstep, all that had been bad enough: but the silence that followed was worse. By October the appalling disarray of the People In Need programme had become apparent in the published accounts: books not kept, bills not paid, writs from suppliers and a deficit – over and above the $2 million released by Hearst and the Corporation – of $350,000. In November, Hearst formally withdrew the $50,000 reward for information leading to Patty's return. The house at Hillsborough was put on the market. Convinced that neither the FBI nor his radical contacts would ever find Patty now, Hearst even accepted an offer from gangland mobster Mickey Cohen to put his 'underworld connections' to the task of tracing her. The deal ended in a humiliating farce when police spotted Mr and Mrs Hearst talking to Cohen at Los Angeles International Airport and stepped in to arrest them for consorting with a known criminal. After being made to stand with their hands spreadeagled against a wall while they were searched, the Hearsts were eventually released, their last desperate initiative in ruins.

The Little-Remiro trial, slated for October, was delayed by defence submissions that the media's mass coverage of the SLA saga rendered a fair trial impossible. It drifted on into the new year of 1975. Known contacts of SLA members – Robyn Steiner, Janet Cooper, Cynthia Garvey and the Halversons – faced continual police harassment and occasional pin-pricking legal actions. Chris Thompson made himself hard to find, emerging occasionally to give 'how-I-knew-the-SLA-but-didn't-belong-to-them' interviews. Thero Wheeler, still assumed by the FBI to have been the second man involved with DeFreeze in Patty's kidnapping but believed to have dropped out of the SLA soon afterwards, stayed in hiding in San Francisco. According to his brother, ironically, a San Francisco policeman, he totally disavowed the SLA as he had a year or two before disavowed Venceremos.

Steven Weed had less and less contact with the family into which he had planned to marry. Always a private man, a loner

– even perhaps, when living with Patty – he withdrew further into himself and began intermittently to write a book on the girl he had loved and lost.

Charles Bates, in the FBI headquarters on Golden Gate Avenue, San Francisco, just down the road from the cobra's deserted lair, kept up the flow of confident messages. In July, 'Time is on our side'; in August, 'People can't stay hidden for ever'; and in October, 'We'll be looking till we find them'.

The excitement of the chase, the 'wanted' posters, were probably all that could keep alive the fraction of a fragment which was what remained of the Symbionese Liberation Army. Even Patty and the Harrises, though drunk on their own 'Butch Cassidy and the Sundance Kid' mentality, must have guessed that their revolution was dead, that the SLA was, despite their brave, defiant words, an army defeated in the field. Their only hope, now that the substance was lost, lay in saving the myth, nurturing the legend, holding intact the mystery. By their disappearance, by staying one step ahead of an ever more humiliated FBI, they might even yet hold the initiative through another act in their masterpiece of guerrilla theatre.

For if it knew and understood little else, the SLA knew and understood the potency of symbolism, the power of the myth. It knew, too, as other guerrilla fighters knew, that a protest deeply rooted in the basic torments of our society – American society, advanced industrial society – cannot simply be exterminated by soldiers or SWAT squads. The killing of George Jackson and a score of Panther activists didn't stop Donald DeFreeze from taking up arms. The Kent State slaughter of white, middle-class students did not deter the white, middle-class girls of the SLA from choosing their path. The killing of one Tania did not prevent the birth of another. The cobra remained, multi-headed, multi-fanged, indestructible.

The SLA's terrible zeal was founded on a burning revolutionary impatience. They could not wait for others to make, as most of them had, the long journey from conservative backgrounds to a new political consciousness. So, denied the mature vision of revolution as an historical process in which many forms of struggle are necessary and valid, they came to believe that they alone were the Way, the Truth and the Life. A one-room apartment became the cradle of the American revolution; a handful of romantics carrying around a jumble of guns in cardboard boxes and an assortment of bullets in plastic bags, became the people's army. In their blinkered world there were few 'people' but many 'pigs' and 'insects'. Revolution itself became less a process of social change and more an adventure in self-discovery, an ego-tripping search for self-purification from bourgeois hang-ups through extreme personal acts of will. And into this matrix of stunted idealism came Patricia Campbell Hearst, rich, pretty, inexperienced – and at war with herself. There was the public Patty: product of Catholic schools, of Hillsborough, of the Burlingame Country Club, of a respected family which automatically assumed its appointed place at the top of American society; the poised Patty, older than her nineteen years, already settled into quiet if fashionably unwed domesticity with a promising young academic. But long before 4 February there was another Patty: the little girl whose teachers had found her a 'strong-minded' child; the fourteen-year-old who, prevented by the nuns from holding hands with her school friends, had found an older man to be her first secret lover and sexual teacher; the independent young woman who, against the opposition of her mother, insisted on embracing the Berkeley life-style, co-habiting with her boyfriend and smoking pot.

It was her inability to reconcile these conflicting personalities – in greater or lesser degree a part of the universal adolescent experience – which stoked up the frustrations, resentments and hatreds which found explosive release (or liberation) in a crowded bed-sitting room overlooking Golden Gate Avenue. Once the brutality of the SLA in kidnapping her had given way to their tenderness in looking after her (and the rapid juxtaposition of brutality and tenderness is a highly charged emotional combination), the path to conversion lay open. Her fears merged with their fears, and their politically-orientated contempt for her parents and her parents' class merged with her own hidden and previously unspoken resentment against a family which she felt had always treated her as a child. Then, when her father's love for her was put to the test, it seemed to her that he failed. Her mother wore black, wept publicly for her poor, lost little girl – and accepted a further term as a university regent. The bottled-up rage against her family, the rage that often accompanies dependency when that dependency is emotional, financial and total, came bursting out – and the emotional storm blew Patty into a new family. Exposed to a barrage of uncomfortable but irrefutable facts about American society and the way of life exemplified by the Hearsts, she discovered a rational base for her emotional metamorphosis. She was no longer a little girl but a grown woman, no longer a helpless victim of uncomprehended social forces but a shaper and moulder of those forces. Her parents had taught her to be a 'nice' girl: the SLA had taught her to be a 'bad' girl, and she liked that better. Steven Weed had given her discreet warmth and decent affection: Willie Wolfe gave her passion and a new name. Patty had submitted: but Tania, with her finger on the trigger of a carbine, would call the shots, steal the headlines, change the world.

The story of Patty Hearst's conversion has been described over and over again as astonishing, extraordinary, unbelievable. But perhaps, in the end, the most astonishing thing about it is the refusal of so many for so long to recognise its inevitability. Could it have happened any other way? Given the characterisation and the story-line, is it credible, after all, that Patty could have remained _un_changed, an unwilling prisoner and unrepentant daughter of the Hearsts?

To millions across America and the world, the story of the making of Tania Hearst will remain the grim, archetypal story of the beautiful maiden dragged off by the mythological beast and unwillingly subjected to the sorcerer's wicked spell. That story, horrifying as it is, is nevertheless more palatable than one in which the beautiful maiden actually _turns into the beast, and does so by her own choice._ So total a rejection, so complete a betrayal, is for most too bleak and terrible to contemplate. So the brainwash theory will never be entirely discarded. There are too many parents – and children – who must cling to it against all evidence. As American columnist Shana Alexander reflected after the Los Angeles shoot-out, 'Part of what makes Patricia Hearst seem so important is not that she is a kidnapped heiress, but that she is heiress and focus to some of our deepest fantasies.'

Somewhere, Tania Hearst is hiding out with Tico and Yolande, safe, maybe, from the FBI but impotent to make any contribution to the healing, cleansing and changing of America. The cobra has devoured six of its children, and smothered the rest.

There will be more cobras, more myths, more fantasies, more Tanias. But the new world of which they dream and for which they rage will continue to be built by the slow, painful, un-rewarded work of the people – not 'the people' of the SLA's abstractions, but men and women who are rooted in their com-munities and work-places, whose consciousness is the product of collective experience, matured in a thousand forms of economic struggle. These people will never be field marshals, nor will their exploits win anyone an Emmy award. But it is their flexibility, their staying power, their collective invincibility which will crush the fascist insect.

'They'll have to kill me before I go back,' said Patty in May. Then there was counter-revolution, then defiance – then silence. 'Wanted – armed and very dangerous' says the FBI. 'We love you, Tania' say the student posters. The power of the myth . .

Chronology

September 1972	'Unisight' (forerunner of Symbionese Liberation Army) formed in Vacaville jail with DeFreeze as leader.
December	DeFreeze transferred to Soledad jail.
5 March 1973	DeFreeze escapes from Soledad and is sheltered by friends.
July	DeFreeze and friends form the SLA.
14 August	Nancy Ling Perry, using alias of 'Nancy DeVoto', rents house at 1560 Sutherland Court, Concord, as SLA hideout.
21 August	SLA try to go public by sending their founding documents and 'Declaration of Revolutionary War' to the press – but they are ignored.
6 November	SLA's first 'combat action'. Dr Marcus Foster killed.
8 November	SLA communiqué to press claims responsibility for killing.
18 November	A further communiqué claims public support for SLA's action.
7 January 1974	Date originally planned for Patty Hearst kidnapping but postponed.

10 January	Little and Remiro arrested, found with SLA literature and charged with Foster's murder.
11 January	Nancy fires Concord house and SLA go to ground.
19 January	Nancy's 'Letter to the People' received by *San Francisco Examiner* (but not published in full till 10 February).
4 February	Patty Hearst kidnapped.
6 February	SLA communiqué claims responsibility for kidnapping and demands that all communications be published in full by the newspapers.
12 February	First SLA tape sent to KPFA radio. Patty tells her parents she's OK and DeFreeze demands massive free food programme.
13 February	Randolph Hearst says SLA's demands are 'physically and financially impossible'.
14 February	Second SLA tape. Patty urges parents to 'stop acting like I'm dead' and DeFreeze presses Hearst for a 'good faith gesture'.
19 February	Hearst says his 'good faith gesture' will take form of $2 million contribution to a 'People in Need' programme.
20 February	Patty's 20th birthday. Third SLA tape, on which DeFreeze demands that $2 million be raised to $6 million.
22 February	First PIN food distribution ends in riots. Hearst says 'the matter is now out of my hands' and passes responsibility to the Hearst Corporation, which promises $4 million if Patty is released.
28 February	Second PIN food distribution.
March	SLA begin to make use of Apartment 6, Golden Gate Avenue, San Francisco, as hiding place for Patty.
3 March	Hearst appeals to Patty to 'get SLA to let you communicate'.
5 and 8 March	Further PIN food distributions.

9 March	SLA's fourth tape. PIN criticised as 'hog-wash' and Patty tells parents: 'I don't be-lieve that you're doing anything at all.'
10 March	Newspapers announce they no longer feel obliged to publish SLA communiqués in full.
10 – 13 March	Hearst conducts secret negotiations with SLA contacts in jail.
25 March	$1 million worth of food given away to 30,000 people in PIN's fifth and final dis-tribution.
31 March	'Death Row' Jefferson and other SLA prison contacts appeal to SLA to begin negotiations for release of Patty.
1 April	Hearst promises an additional $2 million to be paid on 2 January 1975 if Patty is re-leased immediately.
2 April	*Phoenix* newspaper receives SLA note promising details of Patty's release within 72 hours.
3 April	KSAN radio receives fifth SLA tape in which Patty says she's not coming home after all but has chosen to 'stay and fight' with the SLA under the revolutionary name Tania. Hearst family and press claim she has been brainwashed.
15 April	SLA and Patty raid Hibernia bank, Sunset district, San Francisco.
23 April	FBI issue 'Wanted' poster for Patty and other bank robbers.
24 April	SLA's sixth tape. Patty boasts of her parti-cipation in bank raid and derides 'pig Hearsts'.
30 April – 1 May	SLA move from Golden Gate Avenue apartment to Bayview district.
2 May	Police discover Golden Gate Avenue apart-ment empty.
9 May	Patty and Emily and Bill Harris move into new hideout on West 84th St, Los Angeles.

16 May	Shooting incident at Inglewood betrays the SLA's presence in Los Angeles to the police. Patty and the Harrises escape – and disappear.
17 May	Police raid their West 84th St address but find it empty. DeFreeze, Wolfe, Mizmoon, Camilla, Angela and Nancy discovered in house on East 54th St, Compton. Shoot-out and fire in which all six SLA members are killed.
7 June	SLA's seventh tape, from Patty and the Harrises. Patty tells of her love for Wolfe and insists the SLA is not finished.
3 November	After a long, abortive search for the trio, Hearst cancels a $50,000 reward for Patty's safe return.
2 January 1975	Expiry date for the promised final instalment of $2 million to PIN passes without further news of Patty.

INDEX